COLLECTOR'S EDITION
Entertainment WEEKLY

THE **ULTIMATE GUIDE** TO THE **WORLD OF**

# *Harry Potter & Fantastic Beasts*

**IT'S A FLIP BOOK TOO!**
Thumb through the pages, starting with this one, to see the Golden Snitch fly. Illustrations by Martin Gee.

# Contents


4
**"J.K. Rowling's Ministry of Magic" by Stephen King**

12
**Fantastic Beasts and Where to Find Them**

20
**The Fantastic Six**

24
**Reinventing New York**

28
**Magic Across the Pond**

30
**Going from Page to Screen**

36
***Sorcerer's Stone***

42
***Chamber of Secrets***

48
***Prisoner of Azkaban***

54
***Goblet of Fire***

60
***Order of the Phoenix***

66
***Half-Blood Prince***

72
***Deathly Hallows***

80
**Growing Up Potter**

84
**Life Beyond Hogwarts**

86
**Farewell to the Man Behind Severus Snape**

90
**The Future of the Franchise**

94
**J.K.'s Wise Guises**

# J.K. Rowling's Ministry of Magic

## by Stephen King

The master of the modern page-turner pays tribute to the architect of Hogwarts and beyond, musing on her creation and its ability to turn kids into readers.

**AND SO NOW THE HURLY-BURLY'S DONE,** the battle's lost and won—the Battle of Hogwarts, that is—and all the secrets are out of the Sorting Hat. Those who bet Harry Potter would die lost their money; the Boy Who Lived turned out to be exactly that. And if you think that's a spoiler at this late date, you were never much of a Potter fan to begin with. The outrage over early reviews has faded, although the sour taste lingers for many fans. It lingers for me too, although it doesn't have anything to do with the ultimately silly concept of "spoilers."

Jo Rowling set out a sumptuous seven-course meal, carefully prepared, beautifully cooked and lovingly served. The kids and adults who fell in love with the series (I among them) savored every mouthful, from the appetizer (*Sorcerer's Stone*) to the dessert (the gorgeous epilogue of *Deathly Hallows*). Most reviewers, on the other hand, bolted everything down. In their hurry to churn out column inches—and thus remain members of good standing in the Church of What's Happening Now—very few said anything worth remembering. Few really stopped to consider what Ms. Rowling has wrought, where it came from or what it may mean for the future.

So what did happen? Where did this Ministry of Magic come from?

Well, there were straws in the wind. While the academics and bighead education critics were moaning that reading was dead, the kids they were worried about were quietly turning on to the novels of one Robert Lawrence Stine. Known in college as "Jovial Bob" Stine, this fellow gained another nickname later in life, as—ahem—"the Stephen King of children's literature." He wrote his first teen horror novel (*Blind Date*) in 1986, and soon you couldn't glance at a *USA Today* bestseller list without seeing three or four of his paperbacks bobbing around in the Top 50. Like Rowling, Stine was a Scholastic author, and I have no doubt that his success was one of the reasons Scholastic took a chance on a young and unknown British writer in the first place. He's largely unknown and uncredited... but of course John the Baptist never got the same press as Jesus either.

Rowling has been far more successful, critically as well as financially, because the Potter books grew as they went along. That, I think, is their great secret (and not so secret at that; to understand the point visually, watch *Order of the Phoenix* and check out former cutie Ron Weasley towering over Harry and Hermione). R.L. Stine's kids are kids forever, and the kids who enjoyed their adventures grew out of them as inevitably as they outgrew their childhood Nikes. Jo Rowling's kids grew up... and the audience grew up with them.

This wouldn't have mattered so much if she'd been a lousy writer, but she wasn't—she was and is an incredibly gifted novelist. While some of the blogs and the mainstream media mentioned that Rowling's ambition kept pace with the skyrocketing popularity of her books, they largely overlooked the fact that her talent also grew. Talent is never static; it's always growing or dying, and by the time she penned the final line of *Deathly Hallows* ("All was well"), she had become one of the finer stylists in her native country—not as good as Ian McEwan or Ruth Rendell (at least not yet), but easily the peer of Beryl Bainbridge or Martin Amis.

Australian kids feast their eyes on *The Half-Blood Prince*, which went on sale at this Sydney bookstore at exactly one minute past midnight, London time, in July 2005.

And, of course, there was the magic. It's what kids want more than anything; it's what they crave. That goes back to the Brothers Grimm, Hans Christian Andersen and good old Alice, chasing after that wascally wabbit. Kids are always looking for the Ministry of Magic, and they usually find it.

One day in my hometown of Bangor, I was walking up the street and observed a dirty-faced boy of about 3 with scabbed knees and a look of extreme concentration on his face. He was sitting on the dirt strip between the sidewalk and the asphalt. He had a stick in his hand and kept jabbing it into the dirt. "Get down there!" he cried. "Get down there, dammit! You can't come out until I say the Special Word! You can't come out until I say so!"

Several people passed by the kid without paying much attention (if any). I slowed, however, and watched as long as I could—probably because I have spent so much time telling the things inhabiting my own imagination to get back down and not come out until I say so. I was charmed by the kid's effortless make-believe (always assuming it was make-believe, heh-heh-heh). And a couple of things occurred to me. One was that if he had been an adult, the cops would have taken him away either to the drunk tank or to our local Dreamboat Manor for a psychiatric exam. Another was that kids exhibiting paranoid-schizophrenic tendencies are simply accepted in most societies. We all understand that kids are crazy until they hit 8 or so, and we cut their groovy, anything-goes minds some slack.

This happened around 1982, while I was getting ready to write a long story about children and monsters (*It*), and it influenced my thinking on that novel a great deal. Even now, years later, I think of that kid—a little Minister of Magic using a dead twig for a wand—with affection and hope he didn't consider himself too old for Harry Potter when those books started appearing. He might have; sad to think so, but one thing J.R.R. Tolkien acknowledges that Rowling doesn't is that sometimes—often, really—the magic goes away.

It was children whom Ms. Rowling captivated first, demonstrating with the irrefutable logic of something like 10 bazillion books sold that kids are still perfectly willing to put aside their iPods and Game Boys and pick up a book...if the magic is there. That reading itself is magical is a thing I never doubted. I'd give a lot to know how many teenagers (and preteens) texted this message in the days following the last book's release: DON'T CALL ME TODAY I'M READING.

Rowling also brought adults into the reading circle. This is hardly a unique phenomenon, although it seems to be one associated mainly with British authors (there was *Huckleberry Finn*, of course, a sequel to its YA little brother *Tom Sawyer*). *Alice in Wonderland* began as a story told to 10-year-old Alice Liddell by Charles Dodgson (a.k.a. Lewis Carroll); it is now taught in college lit courses. And *Watership Down*, Richard Adams's version of *The Odyssey* (featuring rabbits instead of humans), began as a story told to amuse the author's preteen daughters Juliet and Rosamond on a long car drive. As a book, though, it was marketed as an "adult fantasy" and became an international bestseller.

Maybe it's the British prose. It's hard to resist the hypnotism of those calm and sensible voices, especially when they turn to make-believe. Rowling was always part of that straightforward storytelling tradition (*Peter Pan*, originally a play by the Scot J.M. Barrie, is another case in point). She never loses sight of her main theme—the power of love to turn bewildered, often frightened, children into decent and responsible adults—but her writing is all about story. She's lucid rather than luminous, but that's okay; when she does express strong feelings, she remains their mistress without denying their truth or power. The sweetest example in *Deathly Hallows* comes early, with Harry remembering his childhood years in the Dursley house. "It gave him an odd, empty feeling to remember those times," Rowling writes. "[I]t was like remembering a younger brother whom he had lost." Honest, nostalgic, not sloppy: It's a small example of the style that enabled Jo Rowling to bridge the generation gap without breaking a sweat or losing the cheerful dignity that is one of the series' great charms.

Her characters are lively and well-drawn, her pace is impeccable, and although there are occasional continuity drops, the story as a whole hangs together almost perfectly over its 4,000-plus page length. And she's in full possession of that famously dry British wit, as when Ron, trying to tune into an outlaw news broadcast on his wizard radio, catches a snatch of a pop song called "A Cauldron Full of Hot Strong Love." Must have been some witchy version of Donna Summer doing that one. There's also her wry send-up of the British tabloids—about

Fans pull out the stops for the release of *Cursed Child* (left). A mini Harry lookalike clutches a weighty *Potter* tome (below). J.K. Rowling and Stephen King join forces in 2006 to read from their books (bottom).

> "KIDS ARE ALWAYS LOOKING FOR THE MINISTRY OF MAGIC, AND THEY USUALLY FIND IT"
>
> —STEPHEN KING

which I'm sure she knows plenty—in the person of Rita Skeeter, perhaps the best name to be hung on a fictional character since those of Jonathan Swift. When Elphias Doge, the perfect magical English gentleman, calls Rita "an interfering trout," I felt like standing up and giving a cheer. Take that, Page Six! There's a lot of meat on the bones of these books—good writing, honest feeling, a sweet but uncompromising view of human nature.

Are the books perfect? Indeed not. Some sections are too long. In *Deathly Hallows,* for instance, there's an awful lot of wandering around and camping in that tent; it starts to feel like Ms. Rowling running out the clock on the school year to fit the format of the previous six books. And sometimes she falls prey to the Robinson Crusoe syndrome. In *Crusoe,* whenever the marooned hero requires something, he ventures out to his ship—which has conveniently run aground on the reef surrounding his desert island—and takes what he needs from stores (in one of the most amusing continuity flubs in the history of English literature, Robinson once swims out naked...then fills his pockets). In much the same manner, whenever Harry and his friends get into a tight corner, they produce some new spell—fire, water to douse the fire, stairs that conveniently turn into a slide—and squiggle free. I accepted most of these, partly because there's enough child in me to react gleefully rather than doubtfully but also because I understand that magic is its own thing, and probably boundless. Still, by the time the Battle of Hogwarts was reaching its climax of clumping giants, cheering portraits and flying wizards, I almost longed for someone to pull out a good old MAC-10 and start blasting away like Rambo.

If all those creative spells—produced at the right moment like the stuff from Crusoe's ship—were a sign of creative exhaustion, it's the only one I saw, and that's pretty amazing. Mostly Rowling is just having fun, knocking herself out, and when a good writer is having fun, the audience is almost always having fun too. You can take that one to the bank (and, reader, she did).

One last thing: The bighead academics seem to think that Harry's magic will not be strong enough to make a generation of nonreaders (especially the male half) into bookworms...but they wouldn't be the first to underestimate Harry's magic; just look at what happened to Lord Voldemort. And, of course, the bigheads would never have credited Harry's influence in the first place, if the evidence hadn't come in the form of bestseller lists. A literary hero as big as the Beatles? "Never happen!" the bigheads would have cried. "The traditional novel is as dead as Jacob Marley! Ask anyone who knows! Ask us, in other words!"

But reading was never dead with the kids. *Au contraire*, right now it's probably healthier than the adult version, which has to cope with what seems like at least 400 boring and pretentious "literary novels" each year. While the bigheads have been predicting (and bemoaning) the postliterate society, the kids have been supplementing their Potter with the narratives of Lemony Snicket, the adventures of teenage mastermind Artemis Fowl, Philip Pullman's challenging His Dark Materials trilogy, the Alex Rider adventures, Peter Abrahams's superb Ingrid Levin-Hill mysteries, the stories of those amazing traveling blue jeans. And, of course, we must not forget the unsinkable (if sometimes smelly) Captain Underpants. Also, how about a tip of the old tiara to R.L. Stine, Jo Rowling's jovial John the Baptist?

I began by quoting Shakespeare; I'll close with the Who: The kids are alright. Just how long they stay that way sort of depends on writers like J.K. Rowling, who know how to tell a good story (important) and do it without talking down (more important) or resorting to a lot of high-flown gibberish (vital). Because if the field is left to a bunch of intellectual Muggles who believe the traditional novel is dead, they'll kill the damn thing. It's good make-believe I'm talking about. Known in more formal circles as the Ministry of Magic. J.K. Rowling has set the standard: It's a high one, and God bless her for it.

Fans in Miami (bottom) and Germany (below) attend book-release parties for the *Potter* series. New York readers (left) share their excitement for *Cursed Child*.

**"MOSTLY ROWLING IS JUST HAVING FUN, KNOCKING HERSELF OUT, AND WHEN A GOOD WRITER IS HAVING FUN, THE AUDIENCE IS ALMOST ALWAYS HAVING FUN TOO"**

—STEPHEN KING

# FANTASTIC BEASTS

AND EVERYTHING YOU NEED TO KNOW ABOUT THEM

# SCOOPS FROM THE SET OF THE MOST ANTICIPATED MOVIE OF THE YEAR

NEW CREATURES ✦✦ NEW WIZARDS ✦✦ NEW MYSTERIES

PLUS! PREVIEW THE CAST, SETS, AND COSTUMES

✳ THE MAGICAL SECRETS OF NORTH AMERICA ✳

# PART I

# Once Upon a Time in America

**For her latest fantastical foray, author J.K. Rowling explores the wizarding community of 1920s New York—and some very contemporary parallels—through the eyes of magizoologist Newt Scamander**

**BY JAMES HIBBERD**

Porpentina "Tina" Goldstein (Katherine Waterston), Newt Scamander (Eddie Redmayne), Queenie Goldstein (Alison Sudol) and Jacob Kowalski (Dan Fogler).

**WHEN DIRECTOR DAVID YATES FIRST SCREENED** *Fantastic Beasts and Where to Find Them* for J.K. Rowling, the film wasn't anywhere close to finished. She watched it alone while he waited to see if his team was on the right track. "We were all very nervous," Yates recalls of the private debut in April. When Rowling finally emerged, she found Yates in his editing room. For about a minute, she couldn't say anything. "The film is very emotional," Yates explains. "The end, in particular, is quite tender and moving." And then? "She was very happy."

Naturally, she also had a few notes—she is the architect of the entire *Potter* universe, after all, as well as a producer and the *Fantastic Beasts* screenwriter (her first film script). Nearly a decade after the final book, the author has recently reopened her chamber of secrets, resurrecting Pottermania with a surge of world-building stories on her Pottermore site, her sequel play *Harry Potter and the Cursed Child* in London and now her spinoff film, which perhaps has the highest stakes of all. Can Harry Potter's magic actually extend beyond *Harry Potter*?

Trailers make *Fantastic Beasts* seem like an enchanting romp that follows English magizoologist Newt Scamander (Eddie Redmayne) as he chases the mayhem-causing magical creatures that have escaped his briefcase and are now on the loose in 1926 New York—and that is certainly accurate. But as Rowling's reaction suggests, it would be a mistake to think of *Beasts* as lighthearted. There are some serious-minded undercurrents amid the frantic wand-waving. "There is a dark aspect to it; I think it's going to be surprising how moving it is," Redmayne says, using that M-word again.

And how topical. A film about wizards set nearly a century ago isn't supposed to have much to do with 2016 sociopolitical events, but Yates says Rowling chose the period precisely because it reflected our postmillennial anxieties. After Newt arrives in New York, a series of disturbing events threatens to expose wizards and witches to No-Majs (American slang for "Muggles"). Are Newt's exotic escapees to blame? Or is something sinister going on? To find out, Newt teams up with kindhearted No-Maj

A house elf employed by MACUSA cleans a wand.

Credence Barebone (Ezra Miller) with Percival Graves (Colin Farrell). Credence is the adopted son of Mary Lou Barebone (Samantha Morton), who leads the Second Salemers, a group dedicated to exposing and destroying witches and wizards. Below: Tina Goldstein with Newt Scamander.

**"THE FILM IS VERY EMOTIONAL. THE END, IN PARTICULAR, IS QUITE TENDER AND MOVING"**

**—DIRECTOR DAVID YATES**

Jacob Kowalski (Dan Fogler), deskbound Magical Congress worker Tina Goldstein (Katherine Waterston) and her free-spirited mind-reading sister Queenie (Alison Sudol) while fending off the powerful Director of Magical Security, Percival Graves (Colin Farrell). "It feels like the world is on a precipice," Yates says. "Everyone's a bit nervous. There are things happening that make everyone uncomfortable, and people have a choice to make about which side they want to stand on."

Put another way: Wizards and beasts are being blamed for certain events, resulting in a major cultural debate over whether to demonize them. Sound familiar? "There's a lot about segregation in this film, a lot about fear of the 'other,'" Sudol says. "These creatures, who the world sees as ugly, dangerous or weird—Newt has such love for them, and through his love we fall in love with them. J.K. has tapped into really deep and pertinent issues."

Focusing on that human drama was something Yates continually strove for on the set, according to his cast. "There would be days he'd just say, 'Okay, forget we're all wizards. Forget magic,'" Farrell says. "He just wanted to get to the core of whatever the scene was."

But of course there is magic. As for the beasts themselves, the goal was to have creatures that were largely able to hide in plain sight. The dragon-tinged Occamy could be an exotic bird from the Far East; the Niffler might appear like a snuggly Aussie marsupial. Rowling is already writing a sequel (announced for a 2018 release), which Yates says will take things in a new direction with added characters and perhaps an entirely different setting. "I would like to see Newt out in the wild," Redmayne declares.

His wish could be an actual hint, because the actor knows some of Rowling's closely held secrets about Newt's future. "She comes up and she goes, 'Eddie, I'm not supposed to tell you this, but'—and then she sort of jumps forward with all the details of what's in her brain," he says. "What she's doing gets me so excited." And if Rowling has mastered any real-life spell, conjuring excitement is precisely it.

The goblin Gnarlak (voiced by Ron Perlman) runs a speakeasy. Wizards were not affected by Prohibition laws.

Tina signals Newt to keep mum (left). To play his wizard Doctor Dolittle, Redmayne met with animal handlers to watch how they interact with wildlife. Queenie (Tina's sister and roommate) hobnobs with No-Maj and eternal optimist Jacob (below). Bottom: Newt's mysterious case.

**"I WOULD LIKE TO SEE NEWT OUT IN THE WILD, TO SEE HIM PROPERLY IN THE JUNGLE"**

**—EDDIE REDMAYNE**

The tome that began it all: Harry Potter's original textbook was written by Newt Scamander in 1927 and assigned to Harry in his first year at Hogwarts (right). Percival battles a foe in the New York subway (far right).

Jacob, Newt and Tina on the run (left). Below: Newt prepares a poultice.

"THESE CREATURES, WHO THE WORLD SEES AS UGLY, DANGEROUS OR WEIRD—NEWT HAS SUCH LOVE FOR THEM, AND THROUGH HIS LOVE WE FALL IN LOVE WITH THEM"

—ALISON SUDOL

PHOTOGRAPHS BY MATTHIAS CLAMER

# The Fantastic Six

**From indie darlings to an Oscar winner, these would-be witches and wizards (plus one No-Maj) weigh in on embodying the brand-new crew**

**BY KEITH STASKIEWICZ**
**WITH REPORTING BY JAMES HIBBERD**

Dan Fogler, Katherine Waterston, Eddie Redmayne, Colin Farrell, Alison Sudol and Ezra Miller photographed July 2016 in San Diego.

**1**

**EDDIE REDMAYNE**

The Oscar-winning actor, 34, has had success playing real-life figures like Stephen Hawking and Lili Elbe, but his latest role is almost extravagantly fictional: Newt Scamander, a magizoologist with a suitcase full of impossible fauna. Turns out Redmayne's experience in delicately wrought biopics didn't help much when it came to playing magic. "I don't particularly have a lot of imagination," he says. "I've dreamt all my life about holding a wand, and suddenly I have this thing in my hand and I've got complete stage fright and not a clue what to do with it." Luckily he had a handy how-to in the *Harry Potter* films. "There were specific things that I went and looked at and then thieved," he says.

**2**

**ALISON SUDOL**

Also a singer who records as A Fine Frenzy, Sudol, 31, rounds out *Fantastic Beasts'* motley crew playing Tina's sister Queenie. She works at MACUSA with her sibling and practices "legilimency," a.k.a. mind and soul reading. "She's basically a complete and utter magical empath," Sudol says. "She can read into someone's story, she can see people's goals." She's also the group's resident ray of sunshine: "She's incredibly fun, playful, joyful and free-spirited, kind and wise."

**3**

**COLIN FARRELL**

Farrell, 40, plays Percival Graves, a MACUSA Auror hot on Newt's trail. The Irish star has assayed a diverse array of characters across a thick deck of genres, so you'd think not much could inspire awe in him. But that was before anyone handed the actor a "practice wand" (which he promptly took off-set and back to his hotel room). "I was walking around in my bathrobe with a wand in my hand," he says.

**4**

**DAN FOGLER**

Fogler, 40, is best known for comedies like *Balls of Fury* and *Fanboys*, but here he plays the straight man: Jacob Kowalski, a No-Maj who breaks up with his girlfriend and ends up pulled into the wizarding demimonde of 1920s New York alongside Newt. "[He] gets swept into this magical world with this sense of wonder and openness," producer David Heyman says of Fogler's character. "He's our window in."

**5**

**EZRA MILLER**

Miller, 24, pulls double duty in two of Warner Bros.' biggest franchises: as the Flash in the upcoming *Justice League* and as *Beasts'* enigmatic Credence Barebone, the adopted son of antimagic crusader Mary Lou Barebone (Samantha Morton), whose mysterious provenance will likely prove key. But for now, you won't be able to pull additional details from the actor with a Cruciatus Curse. "If I tell you s--- about my character, I swear there's a sniper up on the roof that will take me out," Miller jokes.

**6**

**KATHERINE WATERSTON**

Waterston, 36, has spent the last few years assembling a lovely bouquet of fine performances in films like *Inherent Vice, Steve Jobs* and *Queen of Earth*—and now makes the jump to high-profile studio fare as Porpentina "Tina" Goldstein, a pragmatic former Auror demoted to a menial position at MACUSA. The actress found herself enchanted by the process of getting into character, especially picking a wand. "You pick up the wand and you feel stupid for, in my case, about three weeks," Waterston says. Eventually "it was so obvious what wand would be right for me," the actress says. "But I did ask for it to be heavier. It just didn't feel powerful enough."

1

4

2

3

5

6

# Reinventing New York

It's one thing to have wizards frolicking around the castles and glens of merry old England, but how do you successfully translate that magical whimsy to the City That Never Sleeps?

**IT TOOK A FULL CREW OF INDUSTRY VETERANS** to turn J.K. Rowling's original screenplay into a living, breathing universe. "It's this fish-out-of-water story of an Englishman in New York," says director David Yates, "and you get this wonderful juxtaposition between the two cultures because there are very different rules and politics in the American wizarding world."

Oscar-winning costume designer Colleen Atwood (*Alice in Wonderland*) says pulling together research for the 1920s was key and asserts that the magical world was based firmly in fact. "It was such a rich period artistically," says Atwood. She adds that Yates "was really in sync with the curious images we found." Even the characters' dos match the clean lines of the film's art-deco-inspired settings. "With the magnificent sets and fabulous costume designs, I kept the overall look of our 1920s New Yorkers very uniform," says Fae Hammond, the film's makeup and hair designer. "Haircuts were uniformly very short."

The film's art department looked for new ways to integrate the story's fantastical elements with its period American trappings. "Throughout, the magical world is grounded in the context of the Muggle world," says Oscar-winning production designer Stuart Craig, "born out of things familiar and real." For example, since Prohibition is in place, Newt will probably have to find a speakeasy if he ever wants to order himself a butterbeer.

—BY KEITH STASKIEWICZ, REPORTING BY JAMES HIBBERD AND DALTON ROSS

To help create Eddie Redmayne's unique look as Newt, Fae Hammond incorporated old faded scars into his makeup, suggesting earlier encounters with magical creatures.

Alison Sudol with Yates (right). Atwood says she took "real silhouettes and expanded upon them for the magical world." Redmayne as Newt on the prowl (far right).

To create the look of Newt's shaggy do, Hammond says they handed Redmayne a wig and a pair of scissors and turned off the lights. "[Newt] would have cut his hair himself in the dark without a mirror on a rolling ocean liner," Hammond says, explaining that the magizoologist would have intentionally planned an inconspicuous arrival in New York (left). Below: Redmayne, Waterston and director Yates.

"DAVID YATES EMBRACED THE TIME AND WORLD OF THIS FILM.... WE HAD A GREAT TIME INCORPORATING THEM INTO THE LAYERS OF THE STORY"

—COLLEEN ATWOOD

# Magic Across the Pond

In her series *History of Magic in North America*, published on Pottermore, J.K. Rowling shared details about the secretive American wizarding community that were very different from the U.K. wizarding world. Here are some departure points.

**THE NONMAGICAL**

In England they're Muggles. Americans call their nonmagical brethren "No-Maj." A controversial law passed in 1790 expanded on the International Statute of Secrecy, instituting "total segregation of the wizarding and No-Maj communities," wrote Rowling. Not only were wizards and witches not permitted to reveal their existence to the unmagical, they were forbidden even casual friendships.

**CURRENCY**

Galleons no more—as of the 18th century, American wizards' currency is the Dragot.

**EDUCATION**

American wizards are taught at the Ilvermorny School of Witchcraft and Wizardry—an institution cofounded by Isolt Sayre, a descendant of Salazar Slytherin, and her No-Maj husband. "The very best of [Slytherin] seemed to have migrated to America," wrote Rowling. The four Houses of Ilvermorny (Horned Serpent, Wampus, Thunderbird and Pukwudgie) were based on Hogwarts's own.

**DARK WIZARDS**

Long before Europe and the U.K. faced the Death Eaters, North America had its own

> "[ROWLING] COULD TAKE A PLACE LIKE NEW YORK ... AND PRESENT IT IN A WAY THAT'S RECOGNIZABLE YET BRAND-NEW"
>
> —COLIN FARRELL

Left, Seraphina Picquery (Carmen Ejogo), the American President of MACUSA; right, inside the U.K. Ministry of Magic.

villains: the Scourers. This ruthless group of wizarding mercenaries took advantage of the New World's lack of regulated government in the late 17th century, becoming a "much-feared and brutal task force" playing on the anxieties of the No-Maj population. During the Salem Witch Trials of 1692-93, "among the so-called Puritan judges were at least two known Scourers," wrote Rowling.

**GOVERNMENT AGENCIES**

Founded in 1693 in response to the Salem Trials, MACUSA (the Magical Congress of the United States of America, pronounced "Mah-cooz-ah") predates the U.S.'s own government by nearly a century. Unlike the Ministry of Magic, it was created as an entity separate from the No-Maj community. In 1920 Seraphina Picquery (Carmen Ejogo) was elected as its president.

**WANDLESS MAGICS**

Only tremendously talented European witches and wizards are able to perform wandless magic (Dumbledore once demonstrated his ability during a Quidditch match). The opposite is true in North America, where it was once unusual to have a wand at all.

**WAND PERMIT LAWS**

Nowadays most wizards wield a wand, largely because they were taught its use at Ilvermorny. Four different wandmakers now call North America home. The use of wands is closely monitored by MACUSA, which, wrote Rowling, is "intended to keep tabs on all magical activity and identify the perpetrators by their wands."

# Going from Page to Screen

Before *Harry Potter* became a blockbuster movie franchise, it was a blockbuster children's book series. Here's the spellbinding story of how the tale of a young wizard made its way to the big screen. – **JEFF JENSEN**

**LIKE HARRY POTTER PEERING INTO THE** Pensieve and finding revelation in a pool of memories, J.K. Rowling found inspiration for her culture-changing creation by looking to her past. She found some of Harry in Ian Potter, a neighborhood kid who used to parade around dressed as a wizard. She found some of Ron in a childhood pal named Sean. She found Hermione—and even more of her characters—in herself, and the joys and misfortunes of a turbulent life. Stuck on a train one night in 1990, Rowling resolved to become the author she wanted to be by gathering these ingredients into a transforming spell. It worked. Later that decade, *Harry Potter* was a rapidly growing publishing phenomenon that was dispelling the notion that kids didn't read and that adults couldn't be equally obsessed with children's literature too.

The magic that summoned *Harry Potter,* the book series, was the total of one woman's life. But it was a kind of lady luck that launched *Harry Potter* as a movie series. In 1997 Nisha Parti, an assistant to movie producer David Heyman, was looking for some weekend reading material. She picked a book from the "low priority" stack of manuscripts the producer was considering to option. When she came to work on Monday, Parti told her boss that *Harry Potter and the Philosopher's Stone* was worth an upgrade to high priority. "'It's a cool idea,'" Heyman recalls her saying. "'It's about a boy in wizarding school.'"

Faithfulness—to the material, to Rowling, to the child actors who would front the franchise—would become the secret ingredient that would make *Harry Potter* magical, inside and out. Heyman would prove to be the perfect Hollywood champion for the franchise: wise as Dumbledore, tenacious as Sirius Black and loyal as Hagrid. He and Warner Bros. wanted to turn every single book into a dedicated movie. It was a risky gambit and an extraordinary show of confidence in Rowling, with only four of seven novels written. They found a like-minded partner in screenwriter Steve Kloves, who was nominated for an Oscar for *Wonder Boys.* He would form a tight bond with Rowling over the course of adapting six of the seven books. "I was really ready to hate [Kloves]," Rowling told *EW* in 2000. "This was the man who was gonna butcher my baby. The first time I met him, he said, 'You know who my favorite character is?' And I thought, 'You're gonna say Ron.' It's real easy to love Ron—but so obvious. But he said 'Hermione.' I just kind of melted."

Next came the director. The producers conducted one of the most famous "bake-offs" in Hollywood history. They met with several candidates—including a famous flirtation with Steven Spielberg—and heard a variety of visions that clashed with their own. Relocating the saga in America. Making an animated movie. Consolidating the three books into one film. (A prevailing attitude among directors ca. 2000 was that the first two books were pure world building, a somewhat thankless exercise for a filmmaker, but the third installment, *Harry Potter and the Prisoner of Azkaban,* was the first truly great yarn in the saga.)

Chris Columbus did not want to do any of those things. A zealous fan thanks to his kids, the blockbuster screenwriter of *Gremlins* and director of *Mrs. Doubtfire* and *Bicentennial Man* embraced a seven-film franchise vision. "I always felt that if you find a piece of material you love, you really shouldn't change it," Columbus told *EW* in 2002. "Had I turned this thing into all the other horrific ideas that were going around—whether I took it to Hollywood

A first edition of *Philosopher's Stone* (later renamed *Sorcerer's Stone* for the American audience) goes on sale at Sotheby's (above). Right: sketches of characters and buildings used in the creation of the films. Gloucester Cathedral (far right) stood in for Hogwarts in some *Sorcerer's Stone* scenes.

J.K. Rowling at King's Cross Station in 1999 (left). Below: illustrations from the interior of the *Harry Potter* books, drawn by Mary GrandPré (see page 33).

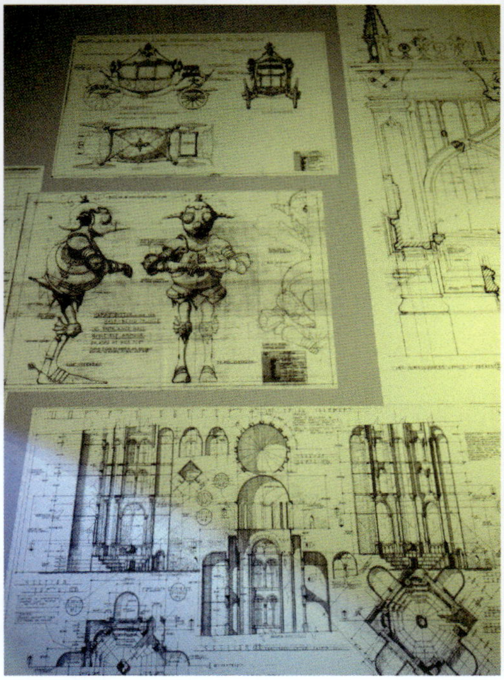

and set it in a high school, put American kids into the production, whatever—I would have been drawn and quartered!"

Columbus envisioned a movie with the grandeur of David Lean's two Dickens adaptations, *Great Expectations* and *Oliver Twist*, with a color palette as bright as *Oliver!* and as dark as *The Godfather*. He brought a number of valuable skills to the task, including an expertise with child actors and familiarity with big-budget fantasy filmmaking. No, he wasn't the prestige auteur fans thought *Harry Potter* deserved. But history would affirm the wisdom of tapping Columbus: He was an ace franchise starter who cared as much about preserving the humanity of his young, vulnerable cast as getting adequate performances from them.

Now all that Hollywood's Pottermakers had to do was actually find those kids. A traditional if unusually high-profile, high-stakes casting process brought them Rupert Grint and Emma Watson. Finding Harry was a more fraught process. Columbus became fixated on Daniel Radcliffe after seeing him in a BBC adaptation of *David Copperfield*, but he was told the boy wasn't available and might be wary of the requirements. Columbus remained fixated on Radcliffe after more searching failed to yield an actor he liked more—and it all worked out in the end. Heyman met Radcliffe purely by accident while attending a play in London's West End (see page 41), and the rest is history.

The perfect casting of Hermione, Ron and Harry set the *Harry Potter* franchise up for success. "It's amazing to me how the development of these kids became the defining story of these movies," Kloves told *EW* back in 2011. "We wouldn't be here without Dan, Rupert and Emma." For Potter's chief cinematic steward, the most anxious moment in the making of the first film was showing it to Rowling. "Nervous as all hell," recalled Heyman. "Afterward she just stood up, walked over and gave me a big hug. To say the least, I was greatly relieved." When everyone else saw it on Nov. 16, 2001, *Harry Potter* fans around the world sighed their own satisfied sigh. The enchantment had begun.

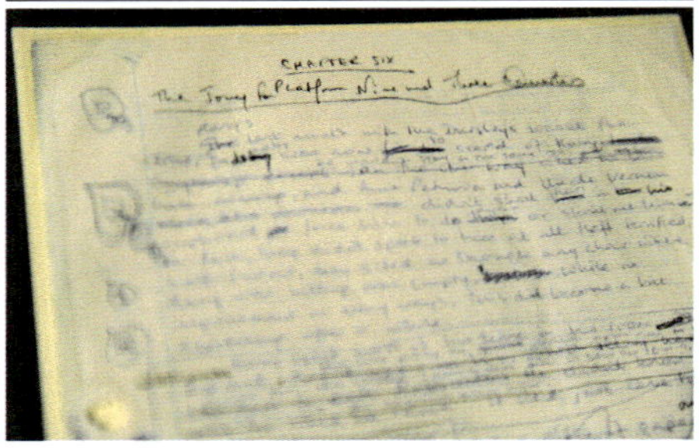

Construction on the set for Bill and Fleur's Shell Cottage in *Deathly Hallows* gets underway (top left). The Nicolas Flamel character was inspired by a real man of the same name who lived 600 years ago in France (top right). Thestrals on set at Warner Bros. Studios Leavesden (above). A Judianna Makovsky design for Dumbledore (middle left). A rare handwritten manuscript of *Harry Potter and the Philosopher's Stone* (below left). Left and far left: color illustrations by Mary GrandPré.

MOVING IMAGES

# PICTURING THE POTTERVERSE

For about a decade, Mary GrandPré was a well-regarded but anonymous illustrator with several children's books to her credit. Then she received a pitch from Scholastic about a young wizard.

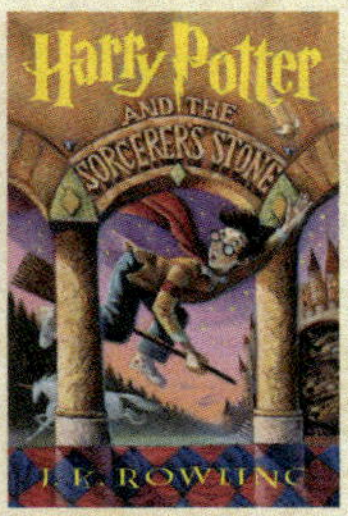

**MARY GRANDPRE** in 2005, with art for *The Half-Blood Prince.*

Rowling may have given Harry life, but illustrator Mary GrandPré gave him his good looks. She's not the only *Harry Potter* illustrator in the world (some foreign editions have covers by different artists), but it is GrandPré's drawings that reach the largest number of readers—tens of millions of Americans—as well as those in South Korea, Poland and Portugal, among other countries.

GrandPré really does know Harry intimately: Only after reading each book several times does she begin to create her signature pastel covers and the black-and-white charcoal drawings for each chapter. "*Harry Potter* was one of the best things for Mary," said her agent Beth Jones in 2000. "But it in no way touches the rest of Mary's talent." GrandPré was already a respected artist when Harry entered her life. So when Scholastic Inc., Rowling's U.S. publisher, asked GrandPré in 1996 to illustrate a book about a boy with magical powers, she thought it sounded sweet. "But I had no idea—no one had any idea—how big Harry would become," she says.

As the youngest of four children, "Mary was always kind of a dreamer," said her sister Linda Riesgraf in 2000. "Even in grade school, she was so much better [an artist] than anyone else her age." After attending the Minneapolis College of Art and Design, GrandPré says she turned down a job as an art director for Hallmark Cards to wait tables and freelance. "I wanted to do my own work," she says. "I wanted freedom." In time she got it. By the 1990s GrandPré had plenty of work, including a job as a conceptual artist for the animated movie *Antz*. "Kids especially are interested in the magical qualities in my work," she says.

GrandPré went on to create covers for all seven books, leaving her mark on *Potter* forever. —CHRISTINA CHEAKALOS, WITH MARGARET NELSON IN ST. PAUL

# THE STORY OF J.K. ROWLING'S HARRY POTTER

## THE SPELLBINDING TALE OF HOW A BELOVED CHILDREN'S BOOK SERIES BECAME A BLOCKBUSTER MOVIE FRANCHISE

---

7 BOOKS | INTO | 8 MOVIES | OVER | 14 YEARS

PLUS! THE KIDS: WHERE ARE THEY NOW?

& FAREWELL ALAN RICKMAN

# PART II

# The Boy Who Lived

**J.K. Rowling wrote a saga that captured the hearts, minds and imaginations of a generation of children—and their parents. Is it any wonder it took an entire country to bring the vision to cinemas?**

**BY KEITH STASKIEWICZ**

Harry Potter (Daniel Radcliffe), Ron Weasley (Rupert Grint) and Hermione Granger (Emma Watson) embarking on a journey that would span 10 years.

**"YER A WIZARD, HARRY!" THESE FOUR WORDS,** barked from the bearded gob of the gentle half-giant Hagrid to the young boy, signaled the beginning of an adventure that would ensorcell millions of people over the course of seven books, eight films and an ever-growing universe of magic and Anglo-inflected wonder. In writing *Harry Potter,* J.K. Rowling didn't just create the bestselling book series of all time; she invented a whole new pop culture mythology, cementing the place of the Boy Who Lived and He Who Shall Not Be Named in the world's shared imagination next to the likes of Dorothy Gale and Darth Vader.

But it wasn't like that back in 1999, the year Warner Bros. purchased the rights to Rowling's world with the intention of bringing it to wider audiences via films. Hollywood isn't exactly renowned for its stringent fidelity to source material, so it was hardly a fait accompli that the studio would turn out a faithful adaptation of Harry's first year at Hogwarts. Fans were concerned: Would they be able to accurately translate indelible sequences like the Sorting Hat or Harry's first Quidditch match? Rowling herself took steps to make sure her creations would be respected, stipulating that only British actors be cast. And in 1999 film officials traveled from the U.K. to the U.S. to make a pitch for the franchise to shoot exclusively in the castles and soundstages of Great Britain. "Harry Potter is something that's weirdly about us—it's culturally British," Steve Norris, head of the British Film Commission, told *EW* at the time. "The thought that it was going to be made anywhere but here sent shudders down everyone's spine. It [would be] like taking *Catcher in the Rye* and trying to make it in Liverpool."

One of the few Americans turned out to be the one behind the camera. Director Chris Columbus (*Adventures in Babysitting, Home Alone*) was a man with no shortage of experience working with young actors, and he came armed with a detailed conception of how he hoped *Sorcerer's Stone* would look. As the first film it would have to serve as the basic story of Harry, Ron and Hermione's

"I'VE ONLY TRIED A FEW SIMPLE [SPELLS] MYSELF, BUT THEY'VE ALL WORKED FOR ME. FOR EXAMPLE... OCULUS REPARO"

—HERMIONE GRANGER TO HARRY POTTER

Wizards throughout the *Potter* series wear glasses. J.K. Rowling was "sick and tired" of only the "brainy one" wearing glasses, and wrote her hero wearing a pair.

◄ **BEHIND THE SCENES** Stuart Craig, the production designer for all eight films, helped create Hogwarts' cavernous Great Hall at Leavesden Studios.

quest to keep the life-giving Stone out of the hands (well, the half-formed head-face) of Voldemort as well as an introduction to their vast, vibrant world. "The inspiration was really from two David Lean pictures: *Great Expectations* and *Oliver Twist.* That sort of darkness, that sort of edge, that quality to the cinematography," Columbus said. "For the color palette, we talked about *Oliver!* and *The Godfather,* which have a sort of rich, almost Technicolor quality to them."

The next big task was casting the series' main trio. Picked from among thousands, Daniel Radcliffe, Emma Watson and Rupert Grint were spot-on ringers for their literary counterparts. (Well, except in one way: Radcliffe didn't have Harry's trademark green eyes and was sensitive to contacts, so his irises often had to be digitally altered throughout the series.) It's especially impressive when you consider that the filmmakers weren't casting just for *Sorcerer's Stone* but for the whole septet of features. In the subsequent decade of production cycles, as their characters graduated from evading trolls in the dungeon to saving the entire wizarding world from the Death Eaters, all three would grow into young-adult professional actors. Eventually, but not quite yet. "They'd throw things at each other and play their Game Boys," said Robbie Coltrane, who played Hagrid.

The rest of the cast was a little more practiced and a little less prank-prone. In fact, the call sheet read like a Burke's Peerage for the British acting community, including the esteemed likes of Alan Rickman as the dour and forbidding Snape, the incomparable Maggie Smith as the protective McGonagall, and Irish acting icon Richard Harris as the fatherly and sagacious Dumbledore. Meanwhile, three-time Oscar winner Stuart Craig was tapped to design the sets, and legendary composer John Williams would provide the score.

The production was ready. Every stone of the castle was in place, the tables in the Great Hall set and the suits of armor polished. The Hogwarts Express was waiting in the station at Platform 9¾. All there was left to do was to capture some magic.

▲ **BEHIND THE SCENES** Chris Columbus demonstrates proper broom technique to Radcliffe. "It was the Chris Columbus School of Acting, which I haven't opened up since," said the director.

► Professor McGonagall (Maggie Smith), in her role as Deputy Headmistress, handles the Sorting Hat as it identifies a House for each First Year.

*Year One*

**Defense Against the Dark Arts Professor**

QUIRINUS QUIRRELL

A young, delicate lad, Quirrell (Ian Hart) elects to voyage around the world before taking up his position of DADA at Hogwarts. When he returns, it is with another being in possession of his body, since Quirrell intentionally sought out what remained of Voldemort. Their encounter results in what J.K. Rowling calls "a frightful mutation of Quirrell's body." Easily compelled by the Dark Lord, Quirrell makes an attempt on Harry's life during his first Quidditch match, seeks unicorns in the forest (to feast on their blood) and finally faces off against Harry in an attempt to gain the Sorcerer's Stone.

RIGHT PLACE, RIGHT TIME

# CASTING DANIEL RADCLIFFE

After an exhausive search, producer David Heyman finally discovered his Harry Potter at the theater—but the future star wasn't even in the play.

Daniel Radcliffe (above left, with Chris Columbus in 2000) was just 11 when he was cast as the Boy Who Lived. He had previously starred with Bob Hoskins in the 1999 British miniseries *David Copperfield* (above right).

In the summer of 2000, the Warner Bros. exec turned producer was preparing to put *Harry Potter and the Sorcerer's Stone* (or "Philosopher's Stone," as the Brits prefer) into production. But Heyman still hadn't cast an actor to play the boy wizard, even after auditioning thousands of children.

One night Heyman and *Potter* screenwriter Steve Kloves decided to catch a production of the Irish tragicomedy *Stones in His Pockets* in London's West End. At the theater Heyman spotted an acquaintance named Alan Radcliffe, who had brought his son Daniel, whom Heyman had never met before. "It was like lightning," says the producer. "I didn't pay attention to the play. I was just looking at him."

The next day Heyman phoned Alan. Tea with Daniel was arranged. There were two other finalists, Heyman remembers, but "Daniel—the way he talked and laughed, and his curiosity—embodied so many of the qualities we were looking for." Radcliffe got the seal of approval from J.K. Rowling as well. "I remember sending a tape of him to Jo and talking her through it as she watched it, and her being so moved by the choice." The rest is franchise history. —JEFF JENSEN

The Chamber of Secrets has
enemies of the heir . . .

# The Trials of Youth

**J.K. Rowling's sophomore offering pushed *Harry Potter* into perilous waters, giving the novice stars the welcome chance to evolve as actors**

**BY KEISHA HATCHETT**

The caretaker of Hogwarts, Argus Filch (David Bradley), encounters Harry in suspiciously close proximity to the message declaring the return of Slytherin's Heir.

**THE PRESSURE WAS ON FOR J.K. ROWLING** when her first book became a cultural phenomenon. After *Chamber of Secrets'* release, some parents complained that the novel (which featured monstrous spiders, Tom Riddle's big reveal and a subterranean cell hiding a basilisk that had murdered a student decades earlier) was far too frightening for young children. Rowling herself admitted the sequel was difficult to write (though she later named it as one of her favorites). Not to worry: The rising stakes didn't deter readers from purchasing tens of million of copies.

Filming for *Chamber* started three days after *Stone* hit theaters, which returning director Chris Columbus said "actually worked out really well, as none of us had the chance to sit back and think about the success of the first film." He added, "I'd felt we learned so much on *Sorcerer's Stone,* and I was so excited about taking all this knowledge into the second film." Subdued lighting and a slightly desaturated color palette, a trend that continued through to the last film, bolstered the ominous mood.

Reviews were mostly favorable for Columbus and his league of extraordinary British actors, including Kenneth Branagh, whom Columbus calls "one of the great stage and screen actors of our time." Branagh had joined the cast as the vain, inept wizard Gilderoy Lockhart. The three young actors were forthright about their developing skills and admitted that they were still honing their craft. Daniel Radcliffe said ruefully in 2011, "I don't think what I was doing in the first two films could really be called acting."

Despite the darker themes of the second movie, the novices as well as the seasoned pros found plenty of lighthearted moments on-set. "A lot of fooling about happens behind takes," said Emma Watson, who recalled a scene in the Great Hall where it was "boiling hot, the food stinks, everyone is dying of boredom and we have to make everybody laugh." The solution? An impromptu cancan and Macarena from Radcliffe, who got up on the table with Robbie Coltrane. "The whole hall was laughing," Watson said.

"I CAN'T BE THE ONLY PARSELMOUTH IN THE SCHOOL. THE HEIR OF SLYTHERIN'S ONE TOO. THAT'S HOW HE'S BEEN CONTROLLING THE BASILISK"

—HARRY POTTER

▲
Dobby, voiced by Toby Jones, makes his first appearance, to warn Harry of dangers at Hogwarts (top). The Slytherin Quidditch team, now with Draco (Tom Felton) as Seeker, prepares to face off against Gryffindor (above).

◀
**BEHIND THE SCENES** J.K. Rowling's inclusion of the blue Ford Anglia in the books was partially inspired by her school friend Sean Harris's vehicle. She has described him as her "getaway driver and foul-weather friend" and admitted basing much of Ron on him.

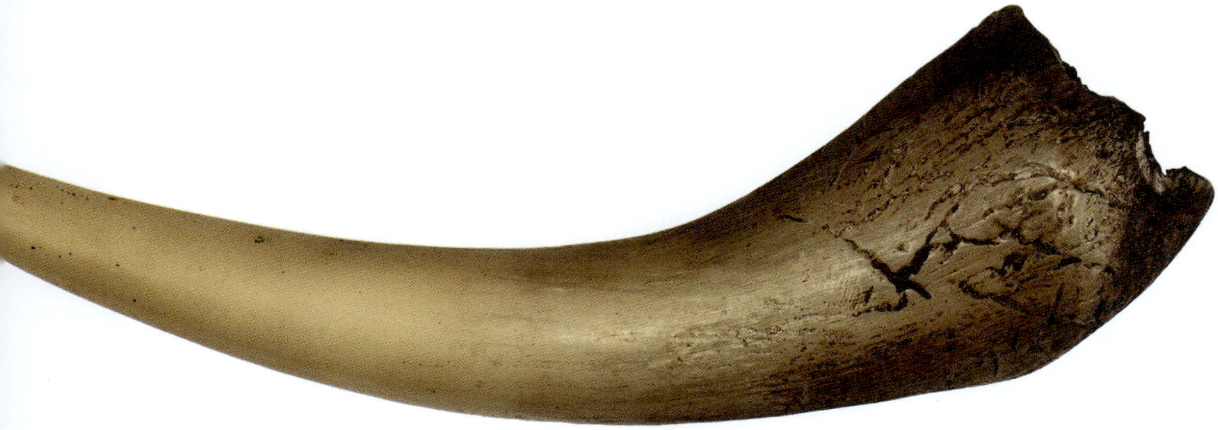

**After discovering Riddle's secret, Harry stabs the diary with a basilisk fang—luckily one of a few objects capable of destroying a Horcrux.**

"Ask [Coltrane] about it. He'll blush!"

Another film also meant another year of growth for the young cast members who were entering puberty. "The hormones had kicked in at this point," said Radcliffe, who, though not yet 13, was considered too hairy for a 12-year-old. One scene called for him to hike up his pant leg to show he's not wearing any socks, and they had to "shave two inches from my ankle," he recalled. There were also budding behind-the-scenes romances that, according to Watson, never actually blossomed. "Those were the days when I had a huge crush on Tom Felton," she said. And was Felton, who played Draco Malfoy, aware of Watson's interest? "Of course I knew," he said. "It was obvious. But I never mentioned it."

It was a stable, nurturing environment for the children on-set, and Columbus and producer David Heyman—backed by a tight-knit crew—shielded Watson, Rupert Grint and Radcliffe from trouble. "There's an awful lot of so-called child stars who get sucked into this business, and the next thing you know they're 15 and in rehab," Coltrane said in 2008. "That hasn't happened here. If anyone came here and said a rude thing about them, I think 300 strong men would leap into action and kill."

Eventually, after much hesitation, Columbus, a father of four, decided he would not return to direct the third movie. "At that point we just assumed we'd be together forever," he said. "I did both films for my kids, but I leave the house at 6:30 a.m. and get home at 10 at night—I'd really like to have dinner with them again!" He broke the news to Radcliffe, Grint and Watson individually.

Though he stepped down as series leader, Columbus continued on as a producer, remaining a member of the Potter family through the final movie. For everyone involved, the experience created lifelong bonds. "Working on *Harry Potter* was so rewarding because you feel that you're part of a great behemoth of a film," said Miriam Margolyes, who played Professor Sprout. "The characters tug you in, into their lives. It's a saga. It's for all time."

▲ **BEHIND THE SCENES** Sculptor Nick Dudman created a 25-ft. head section of the basilisk for the Chamber, which set designer Stuart Craig described as "a Slytherin temple."

▶ Lockhart, a wizard proficient at Memory Charms but not much else, unleashes a horde of Cornish Pixies and, after failing to subdue them, leaves Harry's class to deal with the fallout.

*Year Two*

**Defense Against the Dark Arts Professor**

GILDEROY LOCKHART

Lockhart (played to the hilt by Kenneth Branagh, whom Radcliffe calls "a great bloke") is the five-time winner of *Witch Weekly's* Most Charming Smile Award and author of a series of autobiographical books about his exploits. He joins the Hogwarts staff and appears to be an ideal teacher. But his students quickly discover that his bragging far outstrips any actual skills. Eventually the truth comes out: Lockhart's one great talent lies in Memory Charms, which he uses to take credit for other wizards' victories. A backfiring Charm sends him to St. Mungo's Hospital for Magical Maladies and Injuries.

**WIZARD ARITHMANCY**

# HOGWARTS BY THE NUMBERS

The number 7 is powerful in Potter's world: seven years at Hogwarts; seven players on a Quidditch team; Harry was even born in the seventh month. Here are some other key digits.

## 1 SORTING HAT

Every year, it alone determines in which house a new student should be placed. The head-topper once belonged to Godric Gryffindor, a founder of Hogwarts.

## 2 TRUE PROPHECIES GIVEN BY SYBILL TRELAWNEY

The Divination professor made a pair of correct Second Sight predictions. One told of the rise of a wizard who could defeat Voldemort.

## 3 DEATHLY HALLOWS

As revealed in "The Tale of the Three Brothers," an Invisibility Cloak, a Resurrection Stone and the Elder Wand were given to the trio of Peverell siblings.

## 4 HOUSES OF HOGWARTS

The four founders (Godric Gryffindor, Helga Hufflepuff, Rowena Ravenclaw and Salazar Slytherin) each claimed a house when they established the school together in the 10th century.

## 5 MEMORIES IN THE PENSIEVE

Dumbledore uses the magical receptacle of recollections to show Harry a series of key moments from Voldemort's past. All were drawn from the minds of people who interacted with the former Tom Riddle.

## 6 WEASLEY BROTHERS

William, Charles, Percy, Fred, George and Ron are members of a pure-blood family listed in the Sacred Twenty-Eight, a designation they rejected, earning them the insult "blood traitor."

## 7 HORCRUXES

To defeat Voldemort, Harry and his friends must track down each of these artifacts, which hide portions of the Dark Lord's soul.

# Under A Shifting Moon

**A refocused story line, key new actors and sky-high stakes: With his adaptation of book 3, director Alfonso Cuarón nurtured the series into a startling maturity**

**BY JEFF JENSEN**

Snape defends the three horrified Gryffindors from the werewolf Lupin, who transforms before their eyes after forgetting to take the Wolfsbane Potion.

# The Prisoner of Azkaban

**HARRY POTTER AND THE SORCERER'S STONE** grossed $975 million. *Chamber of Secrets*? $879 million. With magical sums like those, common sense says that you don't mess with your creative potions. But Warner Bros. had no choice as the studio embarked on making *The Prisoner of Azkaban* in 2002. The great Richard Harris had passed away, necessitating a new Dumbledore. Director Chris Columbus was out after an exhausting spell of back-to-back films. ("I was crispy. I was done," he told *EW* in 2004.) And there was a sense that it was time for the franchise to evolve. The first two adaptations were too slavish, too square, too young for many filmgoers. *Harry Potter* needed to change.

Looking for an auteur to infuse *Azkaban* with artistic magic and teach the team some new tricks, producer David Heyman tapped director Alfonso Cuarón. The Mexican helmer only had a few major films to his name, but a couple were widely acclaimed: the lush fantasy-drama *A Little Princess* and the gritty coming-of-age flick *Y Tu Mamá También*. The latter was the better known of the pair, in part because of a much-talked-about ménage à trois. Cuarón joked that *Azkaban* was a natural progression from *Y Tu Mamá También*: "It's the same movie. Two boys, one girl."

Cuarón was an exciting if provocative choice for *Azkaban*, a pivotal point in the *Potter* saga that launches Harry, Ron and Hermione into adolescence. ("Alfonso is basically a teenager himself," said Heyman. "Mischievous. Naughty. Funny. Loves to shake things up.") Rowling doesn't sensationalize the theme in the novel. Teen rebellion is emphasized over hormonal explosion, most notably when Harry runs away from the Dursleys after accidentally using his magic against emotionally abusive Aunt Marge. Harry begins learning to master his anger through a mystery of misunderstanding involving Sirius Black, who allegedly betrayed his parents to Voldemort. *Azkaban* also marked a next-level leap in ambition, tone and stakes for Rowling. The climax was an intricate time-travel caper involving a violent, nearly bone-breaking assault on Harry and Hermione, as well as the wounding of Ron—a rude

▲ **BEHIND THE SCENES** Director Alfonso Cuarón horses around with Grint and Radcliffe at the Leaky Cauldron.

▶ Aunt Marge (Pam Ferris, right), accidentally inflated by Harry while visiting the Dursleys, eventually floats over the town. Unlike Muggle photographs, those taken by wizards move within their frames, like this poster of Gary Oldman's Sirius Black (far right).

Professor McGonagall gives a Time-Turner to Hermione for her ambitious third-year schedule, letting her attend several classes simultaneously. In *Order of the Phoenix,* the entire stock of Time-Turners were rendered inoperable.

"IT IS FIVE MINUTES TO MIDNIGHT. MISS GRANGER, THREE TURNS SHOULD DO IT. GOOD LUCK"

—ALBUS DUMBLEDORE

shock that left fans convinced that Rowling was bent on killing the kid. In *Azkaban*, Harry and friends' experience of themselves and the world becomes more complicated, dark and thrilling, just as it does for many teenagers.

Cuarón himself was a thrill ride, and a disorienting one at first. He wanted to change everything, from the architecture of Hogwarts to the size of Hagrid. The first education that took place during *Azkaban* was Cuarón's: "I had to learn to serve the material and subvert my ego, not vice versa." While the director saturated the movie with impish metaphors for puberty and an abundance of idiosyncratic flourishes, he did so in close consultation with Rowling and submitted to her vetoes. He coached screenwriter Steve Kloves to focus on Harry's hero's journey towards Voldemort and to cut or alter all details, subplots or backstory that didn't nurture that goal. It was "liberating," said Kloves.

Cuarón's other game changers included casting the new Dumbledore, Michael Gambon, who reinvented the part. Gary Oldman, Cuarón's choice for Sirius Black, had a profound impact on Daniel Radcliffe. As did Cuarón. In his first meeting with Radcliffe, Rupert Grint and Emma Watson, the director asked the kids to write essays about their characters. He wanted them to internalize their roles and start acting from the inside out. Radcliffe got to do this during a heavy scene where Harry vows to kill Sirius. Cuarón discussed the meaning of this moment with his young star, then challenged him to figure out how to emotionally connect with the material. "I'll forever be in his debt," said Radcliffe. "It basically affected the way I approached everything after that."

Looking back on the shoot, Cuarón delighted in an experience that stretched him and everyone. "Such a big, beautiful machine. So fun to drive," said the director, who passed on helming the next installment so he could make a dream project, *Children of Men*. "I just hope I didn't jostle the passengers too much." In the long run, the man who made Harry Potter grow up jostled everyone just right.

▲ **BEHIND THE SCENES** In response to Cuarón's request, Watson turned in an 11-page essay about Hermione—and concluded she had a lot in common with her alter ego.

▶ After fleeing 4 Privet Drive, Harry encounters the triple-decker Knight Bus and its conductor, Stan Shunpike (Lee Ingleby). The enchanted vehicle transports Harry to the Leaky Cauldron.

*Year Three*

**Defense Against the Dark Arts Professor**

REMUS JOHN LUPIN

One of the four Marauders (the others being Harry's father, James, Sirius Black and Peter Pettigrew), Remus Lupin is an extremely talented wizard with a dark secret. While we all know what's on page 394, the wizarding world is extremely prejudiced against werewolves, regardless of how friendly they are the other 29 days of the month. Dumbledore persuades Lupin, despite his misgivings, to take the open DADA position. As an incentive, he offers Lupin an endless supply of Wolfsbane Potion, which turns him into an ordinary and sleepy wolf who won't be a danger to any of the children.

CLASS ACTS

# A TALE OF TWO HEADMASTERS

When Richard Harris became ill after playing Dumbledore in the series' first two films, producers were forced to consider who, if anyone, could fill his formidable shoes. Happily, their pick clicked.

Richard Harris

Michael Gambon

Richard Harris initially said no to playing Dumbledore. According to producer David Heyman, the actor's granddaughter demanded he reverse course and accept the role, saying she would never speak to him again if he didn't. Harris relented and donned the headmaster's robes.

Unfortunately the actor's health began to fail in 2002 after filming the first two movies. "I visited [Harris] in the hospital when he was really sick, and when it came time to make the third film, he was clinging on, saying, 'Don't recast!' He was determined to do it," Heyman told *EW* in 2005. Shortly before filming began on *Azkaban*, Harris succumbed to Hodgkin's disease.

The actor was a formidable presence on-set—just as he was throughout his life, when he was as well known for his bacchanalian adventures with fellow bons vivants Peter O'Toole and Richard Burton as he was for such roles as the soulful, singing King Arthur in 1967's *Camelot*. "These were really hard shoes to fill," Heyman said about the recasting. "But Michael Gambon is one of the greats. And he was Alfonso Cuarón's choice."

Other actors may have fretted about filling those magic slippers, but Gambon was game. "I played Dumbledore as I am," he said in 2004. "A little winky. A little like a hippie." Heyman was thrilled with what Gambon brought to the part. "What I love about what Michael did, very early on, was give a performance that paid tribute to Richard by adding a slight Irish lilt to his accent, but at the same time made Dumbledore all his own."

# The Champion and the Spare

**In the supersize fourth installment, Harry endures the terror of an in-the-flesh Voldemort, the fallout from Cedric's game-changing murder and maybe the biggest challenge of all: puberty**

**BY DALTON ROSS**

Harry, transported by Portkey to the graveyard of Voldemort's father, recognizes the names on the headstone and tries to warn Cedric. In the summer before his final year at Hogwarts, Voldemort discovered his father and grandparents were Muggles—and promptly slew them all.

**"I KNEW FROM THE BEGINNING IT WOULD BE** the biggest of the first four," J.K. Rowling told *EW* upon *The Goblet of Fire*'s publication in 2000. "It's symbolic. Harry's horizons are literally and metaphorically widening as he grows older."

*Goblet* serves as a transitional moment for the franchise, revolving around Harry's journey through puberty. "When it's your first crush, it's not just a crush—you looove her," said Radcliffe, on Harry's awkward apprehension at asking Cho Chang to the Yule Ball.

But the real signifier that Goblet is moving into adult territory is the first, haunting appearance of the Dark Mark. The danger ramps up from there, thanks to Barty Crouch Jr.'s impersonation of the new DADA teacher Mad-Eye Moody (see box, page 58), who guides Harry to his graveyard showdown with Voldemort. Screenwriter Steve Kloves described *Goblet* as "the hinge. This one closes the door on everything that came before and sets the stage for a new kind of *Potter* experience altogether."

No wonder Rowling called it "easily" the hardest book to write. The fourth novel even went through multiple titles, beginning with *Harry Potter and the Doomspell Tournament* and changing to *The Triwizard Tournament* before Rowling finally settled on *Goblet of Fire*. The author did massive rewrites of middle sections, which included the excision of an entire character before publication (a Weasley cousin named Mafalda whose story arc was later given to gossipmonger reporter Rita Skeeter, played onscreen by Miranda Richardson).

And, yes, Rowling was as emotionally distraught as the rest of us by the end, when poor Cedric Diggory dies and Harry sees visions of his murdered parents in the graveyard. "It was the first time I cried writing a *Harry Potter* book," Rowling told *EW*.

But there is more to *Goblet* than just emotional doom and gloom. Rowling always used her *Potter* novels to take a not-so-thinly veiled stand against bigotry—the Death Eaters' cries of "mudblood" echoes the dangerous and disturbing master-race vernacular of Nazi Germany—and she expanded on the

▲ **BEHIND THE SCENES** Robert Pattinson (Cedric Diggory) prepares for his death at the hands of Peter Pettigrew.

► Madame Olympe Maxime (Frances de la Tour) towers above her students from Beauxbatons Academy of Magic (right). Draco (Tom Felton) with visiting Durmstrang Institute champion and seeker for the Bulgarian National Quidditch team Viktor Krum, played by Stanislav Ianevski (far right).

The Triwizard Cup, enchanted by Barty Crouch Jr. to serve as a Portkey to Voldemort's father's grave, was designed by prop maker Miraphora Mina to mimic the look of historical relics and chalices.

"WE'LL TAKE IT AT THE SAME TIME. IT'S STILL A HOG-WARTS VICTORY. WE'LL TIE FOR IT"

—HARRY POTTER TO CEDRIC DIGGORY

theme of prejudice by including a subplot in which Hermione fights for the freedom of indentured elves.

"Bigotry is probably the thing I detest most," Rowling told *EW*. "All forms of intolerance, the whole idea of 'that which is different from me is necessarily evil.' I really like to explore the idea that difference is equal and good. But there's another idea that I like to explore too. Oppressed groups are not, generally speaking, people who stand firmly together—no, sadly they kind of subdivide among themselves and fight like hell. That's human nature, so that's what you see here. This world of wizards and witches, they're already ostracized, and then within themselves, they've formed a loathsome pecking order." (Sadly, Hermione's S.P.E.W. story line did not make it into the film. "I was disappointed to hear that," Emma Watson said. "But I guess something had to go.")

*Goblet* also marks the franchise's move into more terrifying territory by giving us the first appearance of Voldemort (Ralph Fiennes) in human form, as well as the Dark Lord's murderous order to "kill the spare." When *Goblet* was first published, there were major concerns from some that such subject matter would be too intense for young readers. But when asked whether she ever considered toning things down, Rowling—who has long railed against those who underestimate the intellectual and emotional capabilities of adolescent bookworms—said she didn't give it a second thought. "The bottom line is, I have to write the story I want to write. I never wrote them with a focus group of 8-year-olds in mind." She added, "I have to continue telling the story the way I want to tell it. I don't at all relish the idea of children in tears, and I absolutely don't deny it's frightening, but it's supposed to be frightening! And if you don't show how scary that is, you cannot show how incredibly brave Harry is."

And in *Goblet of Fire*, whether he was facing a Hungarian Horntail or Voldemort himself, Harry had never been braver.

▲ **BEHIND THE SCENES** The second task in the Triwizard Tournament required underwater shoots. Radcliffe joked that "the hardest thing is you really need to pee all the time."

► Dumbledore attempts to prevent underage entrants into the Tournament by drawing an Age Line around the Goblet of Fire—which works quite successfully against Fred and George.

*Year Four*

**Defense Against the Dark Arts Professor**

ALASTOR "MAD-EYE" MOODY

Dumbledore controversially hires the ex-Auror and veteran of the First Wizarding War. Unfortunately, Professor Moody (played by Brendan Gleeson, the father of Domhnall Gleeson who appears in the films as Bill Weasley) never teaches a single class. His identity and magical appendages (wooden leg and eye) were stolen by the Death Eater Barty Crouch Jr. (David Tennant), who kept Mad-Eye imprisoned. Fake-Moody's mentorship—entirely intended to deliver Harry to Voldemort as a fatted calf—nonetheless greatly affected the young wizard when he suggests to the boy a career in the Aurors.

THE DIRECTOR'S CHAIR

# IN THE LINE OF *FIRE*

British filmmaker Mike Newell opens up about the challenges of adapting the behemoth fourth novel. The biggest? Casting Voldemort.

Ralph Fiennes

**You're the third director to helm a *Potter* flick, after Chris Columbus and Alfonso Cuarón—though you had a chance to direct the first installment. Why did you pass on being the franchise's founding father?**
At the time, I was deep into a film [1999's *Pushing Tin*], and even though it was a completely different story, it had a lot of computer graphics. I had read the first *Potter* novel; it was marvelous, but it was going to be difficult in that technical way, even more so because you're inventing the world. And at that time I was having a difficult time with that same technique. I remember being tremendously conflicted. But the better man did it: Chris Columbus did a heroic job.

**At more than 700 pages, *Goblet* was the first of Rowling's so-called "fat" Potter books. Was it easy for you and screenwriter Steve Kloves to condense?**
Not in the least. We did about 12 formal drafts. A reader can read a rambling narrative like that with great satisfaction, but you can't possibly do that in a two-and-a-half-hour movie. So there was great angst—not only about what one took out but how you gave it a form. That's one of the things I brought to it: This has to be a thriller, driven by Voldemort and his plot to get three drops of Harry's blood to regenerate himself.

***Goblet* has extravagant set pieces, including an undersea kingdom.**
We built a huge tank—far and away the biggest tank for filmmaking purposes in Europe. Dan [Radcliffe] and the other children involved had to do two seemingly simple things: keep their eyes open and their faces mobile enough to express emotion. They're fish, you see—they've been magically given gills, so they can breathe. So there could be none of that "screwing up your face and looking panicky because you're running out of air" stuff. You had 12 seconds before we had to send people down with air masks. We were limited to extraordinarily short stretches of time for each take.

**What led you to tap Ralph Fiennes for Voldemort?**
I wanted Voldemort to be a tremendously charismatic man, and Ralph has tremendous charisma. I wanted to have someone who was entirely cold in his heart, and I knew Ralph could do that very well from *Schindler's List*. And he's a star. He has all the presence and command that a star has. That is very useful for this part. You can't have an undercooked Voldemort. —JEFF JENSEN

# Double, Double Toil & Trouble

The most emotionally complex story of the series, Rowling's fifth book conjured up a major maturation of both character and theme. The movie adaptation landed the bewitching director who'd finish out the saga

**BY KEVIN P. SULLIVAN**

Harry and Hermione, fighting off Death Eaters, are joined by Dumbledore's Army regulars Ginny (Bonnie Wright), Luna (Evanna Lynch) and Neville (Matthew Lewis).

## The Order of the Phoenix

**ONE OF THE COMPLIMENTS OFTEN PAID TO** J.K. Rowling is that the *Harry Potter* series matured along with its readers. Revisiting *Sorcerer's Stone* or *Chamber of Secrets* with a mind toward where the story is headed makes for a nostalgic trip back to a simpler time when no one was dying, no ears were getting blasted off, and owls weren't being Avada Kedavra'd out of the sky. In trying to pinpoint the exact moment of the books' shift from adolescence to young adulthood, there may be no better choice than the death of Cedric Diggory at the end of *Goblet of Fire*. Before then, no character on the side of good had died in the story's present, and the Hufflepuff's murder shades almost everything that follows, but no story more directly than this novel.

When *Order of the Phoenix* (released in 2003) begins, Harry's world has turned a cold shade of blue, a mood literalized in Mary GrandPré's stunning monochromatic cover and the palette of the 2007 film. His friends haven't written. Dumbledore, once his sole source of the whole truth, has withdrawn from him. And after a nearly fatal attack by the Dementors on his aunt and uncle's suburban neighborhood, he's been expelled from Hogwarts. For the extent of the opening chapters, at least, Harry is purposefully led to believe that the life he's worked so hard to foster over the past four magical years has been snuffed out as quickly as Cedric Diggory.

But of course, Harry's isolation has been a ruse set up by the Order of the Phoenix, the clandestine resistance group of witches and wizards established to combat the growing strength of the Dark Lord. Though Harry is finally reunited with Ron and Hermione at 12 Grimmauld Place, a clear line is drawn between the adults of the Order and their children. The trio, along with Ginny, Fred and George, are not to play any part in the fight against Voldemort. But hasn't Harry spent the last four school years face-to-face with dark magic and surviving each and every time—and usually winning the House Cup for that matter? Doesn't that count for anything to these witches and wizards, who are stronger primarily by virtue of their ages? Already

Each of Lord Voldemort's Death Eaters wore a unique mask to conceal their identity from the Wizarding World. Concept artist Rob Bliss created their masks, inscribing many of them with designs resembling Mogul arabesque patterns.

▲
Umbridge sacked Trelawney (Emma Thompson) because she found her incapable of "predicting even tomorrow's weather" (above, top). After a Dementor attack, Vernon (Richard Griffiths, who died in 2013) and Petunia Dursley (Fiona Shaw) comfort Dudley, played by Harry Melling (above).

◀
**BEHIND THE SCENES** Ralph Fiennes (wearing dots used by the SFX team to later render him without a nose) and Michael Gambon prepare for their fight.

"WE MET DRACO MALFOY IN THE WOODS, AND HE GOOD AS TOLD US HIS DAD WAS ONE OF THOSE NUTTERS IN MASKS! AND WE ALL KNOW THE MALFOYS WERE RIGHT IN WITH YOU-KNOW-WHO"

—RON WEASLEY

Harry is butting up against one of the main emotional struggles of the story, the conflicting messages the outside world sends to him and to most teenagers, for that matter: Have a mature and emotionally intelligent understanding of the world around you, but do as you're told.

Thus Rowling has sown the seeds of what she intends for *Order of the Phoenix* to communicate. While it is still very much the fifth story in a series about a boy who goes to wizarding school (complete with all the familiar elements of a *Harry Potter* book—innocent romances, school exams and new beasties), the novel, and in turn the film adaptation, are blueprints for adulthood. Harry, Ron and Hermione learn that the elders in their lives—their parents, teachers and enemies—are fallible. By Dumbledore's own admission, the Headmaster's plan to spare Harry more pain by keeping him uninformed backfires miserably. In Dolores Umbridge, the rosily upholstered Defense Against the Dark Arts teacher (Imelda Staunton), they find the embodiment of power corrupted, the exact kind of authority—prejudiced and cruel—against which to rebel.

The film adaptation of *Order of the Phoenix* brought about a sea change as well, one that would affect the future of the franchise. David Yates, the accomplished U.K. television director behind *State of Play*, would come aboard to steward the series to its bittersweet end, and his first film was a bit of a trial by (magically enchanted) fire. "Jo Rowling has said that if Harry Potter were a real kid in the real world, he'd be deeply damaged, he's been through so much," Yates said. "So I was keen to make this a much more psychological, emotional Harry than we've seen before. Dan's done some wonderful work exploring it, to try to make it real for the audience." Assisting Yates in adapting the largest book of the series was a newly freed-up Daniel Radcliffe, who turned 17 during production and no longer had to attend class while filming. "I'm at a stage now where I'm ready to be pushed further by a director," the actor said at the time. It all added up to a film that lived up to the novel's long, dark shadow.

▲ **BEHIND THE SCENES** Oldman, Radcliffe and Yates prepare to shoot Sirius's death at the hands of Bellatrix Lestrange. Sirius's body is never recovered after it falls through the Veil.

▶ The unhinged Bellatrix (Helena Bonham Carter), who spent 15 years in Azkaban after torturing Neville's parents into insanity, threatens to kill their son.

*Year Five*

**Defense Against the Dark Arts Professor**

DOLORES JANE UMBRIDGE

Imelda Staunton (*Guys and Dolls, Nanny McPhee*) brings Professor (and later High Inquisitor) Umbridge to life in a spectacularly saccharine manner. Her ineffectual teaching style ("wands away") so frustrates Hermione that she persuades Harry to lead a DADA study group: Dumbledore's Army. If you hated her and her Educational Decrees maybe more than You-Know-Who, you aren't alone. Rowling herself admits her bias: "Her desire to control, to punish and to inflict pain, all in the name of law and order, are, I think, every bit as reprehensible as Lord Voldemort's unvarnished espousal of evil."

POTTER IN POP CULTURE

# WE'RE WILD ABOUT HARRY

Thanks to the immense success of Rowling's series, Potter references in the media multiplied as if by a Doubling Charm.

**ENGLISH IMPATIENT**
The Simpsons clan visits London (season 15, episode 4) and runs into J.K. Rowling herself. When Lisa queries about Harry's fate, the hassled author finally gives away the ending: "He grows up and marries you. Is that what you want to hear?"

**MISSION IMPOSSIBLE**
Miranda Priestly (2006's *The Devil Wears Prada*) sends assistant (Anne Hathaway) in search of the still-unpublished *Potter* manuscript.

**LUST AND FOUND**
Lindsay Lohan is more like Hormone-y Granger in an *SNL* sketch (season 29, episode 18) where she has blossomed over the summer.

**BUTTER BEER O.D.**
Simon Pegg stumbles onto *The Tonight Show* (July 28, 2015) as Drunk Ron Weasley and wishes a memorable Happy Birthday to the Boy-Who-Lived.

**YES PLEASE**
In *Yes Man* (2008), Jim Carrey and Zooey Deschanel attend a *Harry Potter* costume party, featuring a costumed Dobby and general awkwardness. —PAUL KATZ

# The Rise of Lord Voldemort

**By the time the sixth movie hit the big screen in 2009, it had been two full years since the release of the final book. So how do you surprise audiences that already know the twists?**

BY ALYSSA SMITH

Bellatrix, celebrating the death of Dumbledore, summons the Dark Mark via the Morsmordre incantation. In the books, its presence is instead bait and cast by the Death Eater Gibbon.

**"I'M NOT GOING TO LIE TO YOU," SCREENWRITER** Steve Kloves said in the months leading up to the 2009 movie's completion. "I do have some concern that because the books are over, the anticipation for the movies won't be the same." Thankfully, that wasn't the case.

The original cut of *The Half-Blood Prince* featured a bold and sophisticated color scheme created by returning director David Yates in collaboration with Oscar-nominated cinematographer Bruno Delbonnel (*Amélie*). Yates said that "we'd done a few wacky things originally"—Daniel Radcliffe called it "surreal"—and eventually agreed to recolor the film at the request of Warner Bros. The result is an eerie, washed-out look well-suited for a mature investigation into Voldemort's dark mind. "In fairness to the studio, they are very sophisticated in their artistic sensibilities," said the director, "but they do have to be aware of what works in the marketplace. I think we've still ended up with a really beautiful-looking film."

When *Prince* opens, Harry is in mourning. His recklessness the previous spring had lured Voldemort out of the shadows and revealed the existence of the prophecy linking their two fates, but at a price: the life of Harry's godfather Sirius. Harry is now heralded as the Chosen One, and for once, *The Daily Prophet* gets it (almost) right. Knowing he must personally kill one of the most powerful wizards alive is a heavy burden, and Harry clings desperately to Dumbledore, the only adult he believes to be capable of facing Voldemort.

The Headmaster encourages their growing relationship by taking Harry with him on trips—first to pick up the new Professor Slughorn (played by the warm Jim Broadbent) but later grooming him to continue the quest for the Horcruxes. "Until now there's been all sorts of talk about finding and stopping Voldemort," said Radcliffe. "In this film Harry starts taking steps towards actually doing that." Their journeys into the Pensieve to investigate the Dark Lord's memories help "illustrate just how much the past informs the present and how much an act of evil can reverberate through the years and affect so many lives," said Kloves.

"SLUGHORN COULD'VE HANDED ME THAT BOOK, BUT NO, I GET THE ONE NO ONE'S EVER WRITTEN ON. *PUKED* ON, BY THE LOOK OF PAGE FIFTY-TWO..."

—RON WEASLEY

**Harry discovers charms, jinxes and hexes like Levicorpus, Sectumsempra and Muffliato written in the margins of a used and well-worn Potion Making book.**

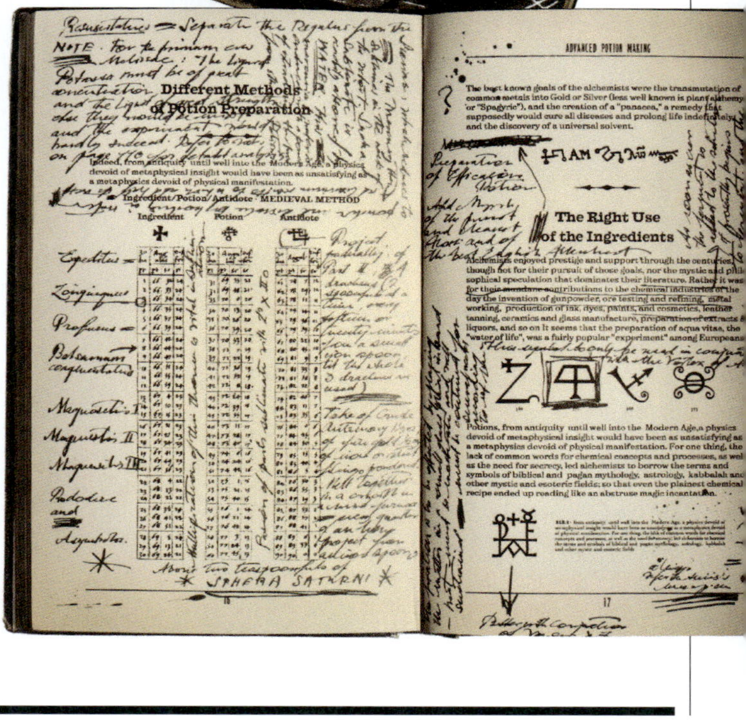


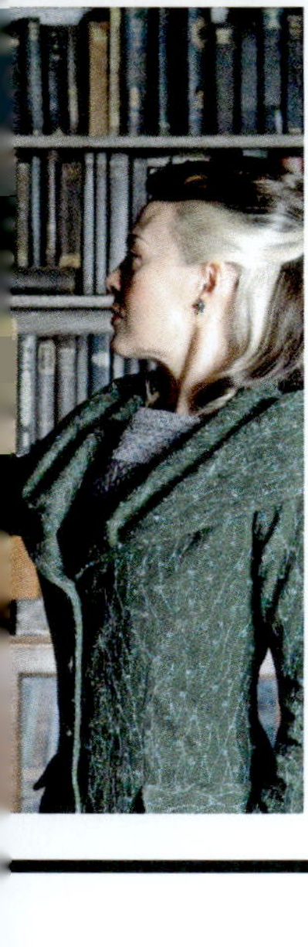

▲ **BEHIND THE SCENES** Michael Gambon wears a green glove on his right hand, which later is digitally withered and blackened. The framing scenes of the cave were filmed at Ireland's Cliffs of Moher.

◀ Hero Fiennes-Tiffin, Ralph Fiennes's nephew, made his big-screen debut as young Riddle (far left). Snape takes the Unbreakable Vow (left).

Voldemort's villainous acts continue to echo throughout Harry's sixth year, as an ever-growing number of parents withdraw their children from school. Yet even as the threat of You-Know-Who looms, classes proceed apace. Ron starts a relationship with his first girlfriend. Hermione worries about her grades. Harry, cautiously optimistic about his future, draws as much joy as he can out of the year: He serves as head of the Gryffindor Quidditch team, discovers an *Advanced Potion Making* book stuffed with secret spells, and begins a sweetly unexpected relationship with Ron's sister Ginny (Bonnie Wright). "This is very much a love story set against the backdrop of war," said producer David Heyman.

Harry's brief moment of adolescent bliss is, of course, doomed; Rowling masterfully foreshadows the book's final showdown in a scene between Snape, Bellatrix and Narcissa Malfoy (Helen McCrory). And even as Harry's star rises, Draco's own fortunes drastically fall. Conscripted into Voldemort's service as a Death Eater, Draco is desperate to complete the impossible task given to him: kill Dumbledore.

Every step leads to Snape's single Avada Kedavra on top of Astronomy Tower, shattering the illusion that all's well. Dumbledore's death is one of the heaviest moments of the franchise and one that deprives Harry of yet another parental figure. At this point in the story, Harry doesn't know that the ever-faithful Snape is in fact following Dumbledore's orders, so Radcliffe had to play the scene carefully. Radcliffe said he found the sequence challenging, partially because there were so many peppy young extras on-set. "[Night scenes] can be quite exciting to shoot because you're up really late," Evanna Lynch (Luna) remembered. "Everyone was just so *not* sad. David Yates was getting quite agitated. He had to remind us, 'Dumbledore's dying!'"

Luckily, the powerful performances of both Radcliffe and Rickman carried the day. "[I]t has many different parts—comedy, romance, suspense, good versus evil—but it also sets up the final chapter that is *Deathly Hallows*," said Heyman. "It really is the beginning of the end."

▲ **BEHIND THE SCENES** Director Yates sits with Radcliffe, Grint and Bonnie Wright during a Christmastime visit to the Burrows, the Weasleys' home.

► Ron defends the Quidditch goal—but bringing the game to life wasn't so fun. Grint said, "Imagine literally sitting on a broom for hours in a big blue room, just on your own."

*Year Six*

**Defense Against the Dark Arts Professor**

SEVERUS SNAPE

Snape (Alan Rickman) finally steps into the position he'd been longing to fill for nearly 20 years. A longtime double agent for Dumbledore against Voldemort's Death Eaters, Snape is a bitter man with few friends who nonetheless manages some heroic acts. The character could have been portrayed as a one-dimensional villain, but at the start of filming, J.K. Rowling shared one crucial detail about Snape's past with Rickman to allow the actor to properly portray the dour, conflicted Potion Master. "I told Alan what lies behind the word 'always,'" Rowling wrote. That was, of course, Snape's love for Harry's mother, Lily Evans.

POTTER'S PAIRINGS

# LOVE ACTUALLY

These five couples didn't need a douse of Amortentia (heyyyyy, Merope) to find their match. They battled Death Eaters, saw their Patronuses change shape and proved love lives beyond death.

**HAGRID & OLYMPE MAXIME**
While the bond between the two half-giants may not have lasted (Olympe objected to Hagrid's dangerous attempts to communicate with his giant half brother Grawp), at least they'll always have that steamy summer of '95.

**HARRY & GINNY**
She had a crush on him for years, but it wasn't until she proved her mettle in Dumbledore's Army that Harry paid attention to her.

**LUPIN & TONKS**
They bonded over late-night missions for the Order, got hitched, named Harry god-father to son Ted and died in battle at each other's sides.

**BILL & FLEUR**
It took Bill being disfigured by a werewolf before Molly Weasley embraced Fleur, who said, "I am good-looking enough for the both of us!"

**RON & HERMIONE**
The big kiss happened when Ron thought to rescue the house-elves prior to the Battle of Hogwarts. What can we say? He's a Keeper.

# Hunt for the Horcruxes

**It all comes down to this. The final book gets an explosive two-parter featuring Harry, Hermione and Ron on the run from Lord Voldemort and the Death Eaters**

**BY KEITH STASKIEWICZ**

During the Battle of the Seven Potters, the Order of the Phoenix uses Polyjuice to confuse the Death Eaters. The real Harry is paired with Hagrid, who once brought the boy as an infant to the Dursleys' house on the same motorbike.

**WHEN YOU THINK ABOUT IT, THERE'S NO** greater or more effective real-world Horcrux than a work of art. There's little doubt that J.K. Rowling hid a slice of her soul in each of the seven books she wrote for the series, ensuring that her spirit would live on long after her death. But even mega-massively popular story cycles must come to an end. While readers were treated to—and wept along with—Harry & Co.'s denouement in 2007 with the release of Rowling's last book, it took another four years before the Hogwarts Express rumbled into its true terminus with the last film, *Harry Potter and the Deathly Hallows—Part 2.*

The end was always right there in the beginning. The story may have ballooned and spun out in unexpected ways over the years—at the very least the Black family tree did—but the core conflict was the same: Harry vs. Voldemort, Good vs. Evil, Life vs. Death. Rowling always knew she wanted a book for each year at Hogwarts and no more; it just turned out that the hardest lesson the school had to teach us was how to say goodbye.

Fourteen years had passed between the publication of the first book and the release of the last film. For the first time in that span, audiences were being faced with the daunting prospect of no new Potter on the horizon. The difficulty of letting go was evidenced by the decision to split the book into two final films—a Part 1 and Part 2. This stab at prolongation gave the filmmakers extra runway with which to depict the epic climactic showdown as well as extra time for the studio to come to grips with the end of its *Potter* blockbusters.

David Yates, who had directed both *Order of the Phoenix* and *Half-Blood Prince*, would shepherd the series to its finish, filming the bifurcated finale back-to-back during a grueling production. "We shot for a very long time, by any standards," Yates told *EW*. "There were phases, periods, where they all felt like, 'God, we just gotta get to the end of it. We need closure.'" *Deathly Hallows* starts with Harry, Ron and Hermione in hiding, searching

▲ **BEHIND THE SCENES** Ron got "splinched" (a common side effect from a failed apparition) when fleeing the Ministry of Magic. Here, makeup artists create the wound.

► To break into Bellatrix's vault at Gringotts, Harry, Hermione and Ron face the Thief's Downfall (a waterfall that washes away any enchantment); Geminio and Flagrante curses (everything in the vault multiplies into worthless copies—and burns); and a half-blind Ukrainian Ironbelly dragon.

▲
The Gringotts bank tellers were created using practical effects on real actors. Pictured on left: Rusty Goffe, who played one of the goblins (top). Hermione stands in the snowy woods where she, Harry and Ron camped during quest for the Horcruxes (middle). Lucius Malfoy, recently escaped from Azkaban, hosts a gathering of Death Eaters at his family mansion (bottom).

for Voldemort's hidden Horcruxes. White-knuckled break-ins to both the Ministry of Magic and Gringotts Bank serve as appetizers for the series' final—and biggest—action sequence: the endgame battle between Dumbledore's Army and the Death Eaters. It's a fight that takes up most of the running time of the second film as well as one that not every character survives. (R.I.P., Remus Lupin—you were too good for this world.)

The dead weren't the only goodbyes that needed to be said. As the filmmakers and cast wrapped up a decade of work, putting props back in their boxes and pulling tarpaulins over sets they'd used for eight feature films, the full weight of the accomplishment hit them. "Somehow I wasn't prepared for how emotional it was," Rupert Grint said. "It hit home how much it all meant to us." By this point Grint, Radcliffe and Watson had been playing their characters for nearly half their lives. "*Harry Potter* has given me everything," said Radcliffe at the time. "I'll always be grateful for it." Watson was more pragmatic about arriving at their journey's conclusion. "The three of us were just in pieces by the end. It was our lives played over on tape, and all these people that we've known, in this place where we'd spent more time than in our actual homes. It was overwhelming."

But *Deathly Hallows* is, among other things, a story about acceptance. Harry dies at the climax, returning to life only when he comes to terms with his own mortality. It is Voldemort's desire to master the forces of death that is his great curse and undoing. Rowling knew how difficult it would be for the world to bid adieu to this beloved universe she had created, and there certainly was plenty of weeping and gnashing of teeth when Potter fans realized the pipeline was dry and the saga of the Boy Who Lived versus He-Who-Must-Not-Be-Named was truly at an end. But there was also the sense of completion and satisfaction that comes at the tail end of a story well told—a sense that, to borrow Rowling's reassuring final line, all was well.

▲ **BEHIND THE SCENES** (From left) Director David Yates with first A.D. Jamie Christopher, David Thewlis (Lupin), Daniel Radcliffe and James Phelps (Fred) on the *Deathly Hallows* set.

▶ Neville Longbottom fit every criterion of Trelawney's prophecy save one: Voldemort did not mark him as an equal. He might have made a mistake. Neville defies the Dark Lord and earns Godric's sword—which he promptly uses to destroy the last Horcrux (right). Molly Weasley (Julie Walters) dueling Bellatrix—and winning (far right).

Harry's wand (left) and Voldemort's (middle) shared a common core: a feather donated from Fawkes. After Voldemort's wand failed him, he sought the Elder Wand (right) and found it in Dumbledore's grave.

"HE WANTED TO KNOW EVERYTHING I COULD TELL HIM ABOUT THE WAND VARIOUSLY KNOWN AS THE DEATHSTICK, THE WAND OF DESTINY OR THE ELDER WAND"

—OLLIVANDER TALKING ABOUT VOLDEMORT

SEEING DOUBLE

# WHY THEY HALVED *HALLOWS*

After reading *Harry Potter and the Deathly Hallows*, film producer David Barron struggled with how to wrangle such a behemoth into a single film. His solution surprised even him.

D David Barron immediately e-mailed fellow producer David Heyman. They both pondered the breadth of the project ahead of them. "My God, this is a big film," said Barron. Heyman replied, "The biggest." Then came the suggestion from Barron that changed everything: "Maybe even two."

Eventually it was decided: *Hallows* would be split into a two-part cinematic event. "I ultimately realized: What do you cut?" Heyman said. At the time, there was a rumor the choice was made for profit, but Heyman said, "I promiseyoupromiseyoupromiseyou, it was all about making the best possible version of that book."

Despite the filmmakers' insistence that the choice to split the films was made to be as faithful to the books as possible, some skeptical fans believe the decision was made for purely commercial reasons. "The key word there is 'purely,'" said Warner Bros. Entertainment president Alan Horn. "I don't want to be disingenuous or dishonest about this. There's no question that Warner Bros. will make more money with two films than they would have with one. But we also never, ever would have done this if Jo [Rowling] had not endorsed it and if we didn't feel that we were providing a better finale, with a more full sense of closure. We just respect and love the books too much for that." —JEFF JENSEN AND SEAN SMITH

▲ Harry and Voldemort meet for the last time in the Hogwarts courtyard. Production designer and three-time Oscar winner Stuart Craig (*The English Patient, Gandhi, Dangerous Liaisons*) created the set at Leavesden Studios. "You can't just go around punching holes in sets," he said. "You'll just get a lot of visible Styrofoam and plaster." The production team worked nonstop to create faux stones and rubble from polystyrene.

◄ McGonagall (Maggie Smith) views the wreckage. The actress said she won't miss filming: "It was 10 years, and that's a lot" (far left). Dumbledore meets Harry one last time at a ghostly King's Cross Station. Unlike in the book, Harry is fully clothed. "I thought it would be a tad distracting otherwise," said director Yates (left).

# Growing Up Potter

Over the span of a decade, the three adorably precocious British tots flourished and blossomed, growing up to become superstars in their own right. —BY JEFF JENSEN

**THE FIRST SCENE DANIEL RADCLIFFE EVER** shot as Harry Potter was the very last scene in *Harry Potter and the Sorcerer's Stone*. It was Oct. 2, 2000, in Goathland, England, a tiny village whose quaint railway stop doubled as Hogsmeade Station. On his first day wearing the boy wizard's glasses and lightning-bolt scar, the 11-year-old Londoner had to board the Hogwarts Express alongside Rupert Grint and Emma Watson. Radcliffe was no stranger to movie sets; he had just made *David Copperfield* and *The Tailor of Panama*. And yet his previous experience could not prepare him for the moment when he saw a mob of extras—150 kids, all dressed in Hogwarts robes—staring in their direction. In that instant, Radcliffe says, he felt most unmagical. "I remember everyone looking at us and going, 'Oh my God. That's him,'" recalled the actor in 2011. "I was a kid among other kids. To be 'special' just because I had been picked for this part was just…bizarre."

While the *Potter* films brought Radcliffe fame and riches, what's remarkable is how he used his decade of playing Harry to stretch as a person and as an actor. His defining memories of the franchise aren't about filming Quidditch scenes or kissing Bonnie Wright. Instead he remembers how Alfonso Cuarón instilled in him a passion for cinema, or the time Gary Oldman taught him the bass line to the Beatles' "Come Together." In 2007 Radcliffe spent his break between *Potter* films laying himself bare—emotionally and physically—in an acclaimed London

Emma Watson, Rupert Grint and Daniel Radcliffe in 2005, prior to the release of *Goblet of Fire*.

PHOTOGRAPH BY AMY GUIP

Clockwise from above: The trio stand with Robbie Coltrane (left), Rowling (middle) and Kenneth Branagh (right) in 2002 at a *Chamber of Secrets* event; the stars with Rowling at the world premiere of *Deathly Hallows: Part 2* in 2011; Watson and Grint meet Cher in 2001.

stage revival of *Equus* (he brought the role to Broadway the following year).

He's the first to admit he might not be the right fit for most studio blockbusters ("At 5'5", I am not a natural action-movie star"), but that hasn't stopped him from developing an eclectic post-*Potter* career. Mentioning an interest to work on "smaller things for a while," Radcliffe appeared on Broadway in 2011-2012 in the musical *How to Succeed in Business Without Really Trying* and in artsy films like 2013's *Horns*, as well as experimenting with roles in traditional Hollywood blockbusters like 2016's *Now You See Me 2*. "We were so proud of Dan," said *Potter* producer David Barron. "He has such a huge appetite to learn and grow. It was the same kind of pride as watching your own children flourish."

Radcliffe—who completed his formal education via tutors—credits his costars for his personal growth, citing in particular the brother-sister relationship with Emma Watson. They certainly argued like siblings—but in a good way, about politics, religion and art. Said Watson: "William Blake, who is one of my favorite poets, wrote, 'Without contraries is no progression.' Dan and I, we really sparked on each other. He questioned me. He made me think. He's so incredibly driven, ambitious and passionate. You get something when you're around someone like that all the time. He gives you that energy. I will miss that. A lot."

As for Watson herself, it was clear the 9-year-old was just as capable and precocious as the future Mrs. Ron Weasley. "There was no question," said director Chris Columbus, who cast her. "She was Hermione." Today the sophisticated little girl (who used to decorate her dressing room with stuffed animals) is a sophisticated young woman who was appointed a U.N. Women Goodwill Ambassador in 2014 and stumps for fair trade. "I have spent more of my life being someone else than I have being myself," said Watson in 2011. She famously commemorated the end of *Potter* by adopting a stylish pixie hairdo. "I've always had a strong sense of who I am, of what I want, but I do need to spend more time figuring that out."

There was a time when Watson wasn't sure she wanted to be an actress. Of the three *Potter* leads, she took the longest to sign a contract to do the last three films. But now she seems much more content to continue down the path. Her widely anticipated appearance as Belle in the live-action *Beauty and the Beast* hits screens in 2017. Past films have included 2012's *The Perks of Being a Wallflower* and 2015's *Colonia*. "I want to choose projects that mean something to me," Watson said, acknowledging

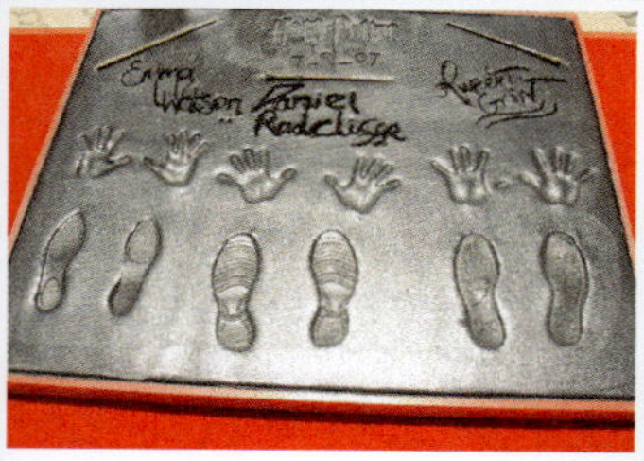

In 2012 Radcliffe appeared on *SNL* (top) and joked, "Let's not do [any *Potter* sketches]," as cast members appeared behind him dressed as familiar characters. The actors graced the cover of *Life* in 2005 (right) and in 2007 left their hand, foot and wand prints in Hollywood at Grauman's Chinese Theatre (above).

**"I HAVE SPENT MORE OF MY LIFE BEING SOMEONE ELSE THAN I HAVE BEING MYSELF"**

**—EMMA WATSON**

that her *Potter* paychecks enable her to be pickier than most young stars. "Film is an incredibly powerful medium, and filmmakers have the power to affect the way people think about the future. I would love to play a part in that. I don't know everything," she said matter-of-factly. "I have so much to learn. And I couldn't be more excited about that."

And Rupert Grint? Those who know him will tell you about his pet teacup pigs, the Mr. Whippy ice cream truck he drives around for fun, his passion for the art of the late curly-haired PBS painting instructor Bob Ross. "I've never been to Rupert's house," said Radcliffe in 2011, "but I've always imagined it to be a little like Pee-wee Herman's home. I just picture him waking up every morning, then sliding down a waterslide to the breakfast table."

"I have always enjoyed things that are a little different, a little odd," Grint admitted at that time. He's chosen his non-*Potter* roles accordingly. The actor appeared in several British indie films, including the edgy drama *Cherrybomb* (2009) and the action comedy *Wild Target* (2010). It was "just for fun, really," said Grint. "And probably for my sanity, too." His post-*Potter* career includes movies like 2015's *Moonwalkers*, and he's currently attached to two 2017 TV series, *Snatch* and *Sick Note*.

"He has the nicest nature of anyone I have ever met," said Watson. "So down-to-earth. So solid. He's my rock." Perhaps that's part of what makes him so well attuned to his feelings—especially about leaving the world of Harry Potter behind. "I was quite relieved when we wrapped," the actor said. "But I felt an overwhelming sadness as well. I do miss it. It's going to take a while to move on."

# Life Beyond Hogwarts

After passing their O.W.L.s and N.E.W.T.s, these talented young actors went on to land impressive roles on screens and stages. —ALYSSA SMITH

**1**

**ROBERT PATTINSON (CEDRIC DIGGORY)**

*COSMOPOLIS*, 2012

Three years after he starred in *Potter*, Pattinson landed the role of a lifetime as Edward in *Twilight*. His later career includes indie films like this Cannes drama.

**2**

**EVANNA LYNCH (LUNA LOVEGOOD)**

*G.B.F.*, 2013

The Irish actress memorably revisited her *Potter* role in Darren Criss and StarKid's unofficial musical *A Very Potter Senior Year* during 2013's Leakycon. She's picked up roles in indie teen films, including *G.B.F.* and *My Name Is Emily* (2015).

**3**

**MATTHEW LEWIS (NEVILLE LONGBOTTOM)**

*ME BEFORE YOU*, 2016

The *Potter* hottie memorably took his shirt (and pants) off for a cover of the British magazine *Attitude* and appeared on TV and a romantic film, here opposite Emilia Clarke.

**4**

**TOM FELTON (DRACO MALFOY)**

*RISEN*, 2016

He went bananas in *Rise of the Planet of the Apes*, then explored the origins of Christianity opposite former costar Ralph Fiennes's bro Joseph.

**5**

**KATIE LEUNG (CHO CHANG)**

*ONE CHILD*, 2014

Potter's former sweetheart has spent time on the stage, including a 2012 run of Jung Chang's bestselling memoir *Wild Swans*, and starred in this BBC drama miniseries.

**6**

**DOMHNALL GLEESON (BILL WEASLEY)**

*STAR WARS: THE FORCE AWAKENS*, 2015

Nominated for a Tony Award before he even set foot on the *Potter* set, Gleeson continues to rack up roles, including an impressive four movies in 2015: *Ex Machina*, *Brooklyn*, *The Revenant* and *The Force Awakens*.

**7**

**ALFRED ENOCH (DEAN THOMAS)**

*HOW TO GET AWAY WITH MURDER*, 2014

Following a string of guest roles on TV shows, including *Sherlock* in 2014, the former school rower struck gold on this Shonda Rhimes hit.

**8**

**BONNIE WRIGHT (GINNY WEASLEY)**

*BEFORE I SLEEP*, 2013

In addition to roles in movies like this indie drama, Wright presented her directorial debut, the coming-of-age *Separate We Come, Separate We Go*, at Cannes in 2012.

1

2

3

4

"I GOT [THE ROLE OF BILL] BECAUSE I'M A GINGER"

—DOMHNALL GLEESON

"[THE FILMS] INSPIRED ME TO FOLLOW MY DREAMS AND KEEP ACTING AND MAKING MOVIES"

—BONNIE WRIGHT

# Farewell to the Man Behind Severus Snape

Alan Rickman may have been best known for playing complex and effortlessly self-possessed baddies. But the actor, who died at age 69, was cherished by those who worked with him for his innate goodness —CHRIS NASHAWATY

**ON JAN. 14, 2016, THE WORLD OF HOGWARTS** (and beyond) lost one of its most memorable and magical figures when Rickman died from cancer. With his sleepy-lidded dark eyes and impossibly deep purr of a voice that infused every utterance with creepy insinuation, the acclaimed British actor, who brought the role of the sinister-seeming Severus Snape to life in all eight Harry Potter films, left behind an indelible legacy. He was the man Muggle moviegoers loved to hate—and, perhaps against their better judgment, hated to love.

In the days after his untimely death, the Potter faithful transformed Platform 9¾ at London's King's Cross Station into a makeshift memorial, leaving behind flowers and handwritten notes. Meanwhile, J.K. Rowling paid tribute, calling Rickman a "magnificent and wonderful man." Emma Watson added, "I feel so lucky to have worked and spent time with such a special man and actor." Not surprisingly it was Daniel Radcliffe, whose boy wizard squared off against Hogwarts' Professor of Potions for nearly a decade, who offered the most heartfelt tribute, recalling how Rickman was one of the first adults to treat him like a peer rather than a child. "Alan Rickman is undoubtedly one of the greatest actors I will ever work with," wrote Radcliffe. "People create perceptions of actors based on the parts they played, so it might surprise some people to learn that contrary to some of the sterner (or downright scary) characters he played, Alan was extremely kind, generous, self-deprecating and funny."

Early on, though, Rickman's young costars weren't so sure. "Alan definitely had his own type of villainy about him," said Tom Felton (Draco). He'd certainly had enough practice. Trained at London's Royal Academy of Dramatic Art, Rickman spent the first part of his career onstage, where he earned a Tony nomination for his devilishly lusty performance as the Vicomte de Valmont in 1987's *Les Liaisons Dangereuses.* It wasn't until the following year that he made his movie debut (at age 42!) as Hans Gruber, *Die Hard*'s sharply dressed German terrorist. Over the next two decades, Rickman would assemble an all-star gallery of rogues in such films as *Robin Hood: Prince of Thieves* and *Sweeney Todd.* No one was as good at being bad.

Still, it was his deceptively layered and darkly wicked turn as Snape—a character who oozed both menace and moral rot—that introduced him to a new generation, providing him with the most iconic role of his career. Just try to go back and reread Rowling's books without hearing Rickman's voice in your head. It's impossible. For some actors, that sort of identification with a character may seem like a prison. Not Rickman. When *Deathly Hallows—Part 2* wrapped in 2011, he wrote a letter describing the pleasure of having seen the young cast grow into young men and women of accomplishment and poise. "A lifetime seems to have passed in minutes," he wrote with paternal pride. Later, at the film's premiere, Rickman was asked to sum up his feelings about the decade-long saga that cast a spell like no other. In that inimitable voice, he replied, "I think things like this are meant to end, and you should not miss it—you should just be happy that it ends well."

Rickman attending a "Meet the Filmmaker" special in New York on June 19, 2015.

**"ALAN RICKMAN WAS ACTUALLY ONE OF THE FEW THAT I WAS NERVOUS AROUND....IT TOOK ME ABOUT FIVE YEARS TO MUSTER UP A CONVERSATION WITH HIM"**

—TOM FELTON

# POTTERMANIA RETURNS

## HOW J.K. ROWLING CREATED A NEVER-ENDING WORLD OF ENCHANTMENT THAT CHARMED A GENERATION

---

- THE WIZARDING WORLD
- VIDEO GAMES
- THE LATEST TOYS

---

## PLUS! *CURSED CHILD* COMMANDS THE STAGE

***HARRY POTTER*** **AUTHOR REIGNS ON TWITTER**

PART III

# The Future of the Franchise

The Dark Lord had fallen—both on the page and onscreen—and all was well for the Boy Who Lived, but the saga continues in other media, eras and continents.
**—BY KEVIN SULLIVAN**

**SEVEN YEARS. SEVEN BOOKS. THAT WAS THE** promise J.K. Rowling made to her readers, giving us plenty of time to prepare for the inevitably bittersweet end. And yet, how could there not be more? The richness of Rowling's writing style hinted at deeper layers beneath the surface—there's always another secret Hogwarts corridor to explore, always another buried story to unearth. But when *Harry Potter and the Deathly Hallows* hit shelves in 2007, readers had to admit that this would be it…right?

To fill the immediate void, fans stepped in. In 2009 future *Glee* star Darren Criss starred in *A Very Potter Musical,* a song-and-dance reimagining of Rowling's world, and fan fiction flourished. As did tech products: Video games and eventually smartphone apps hit the market. When the Wizarding World of Harry Potter opened at Universal Studios, Florida, in 2010, we Muggles could finally approximate the thrill of visiting Ollivanders' wand shop and drinking butterbeers at Hog's Head. (A second park, in Los Angeles, opened in 2016.)

All the while, Rowling kept largely to herself until out of the blue one day in 2011, she launched Pottermore. Initially an online platform for the release of Harry Potter e-books, it came with the author's promise of new material set within the wizarding universe. There were short stories and wizarding world "news" articles, all written by Rowling, that dazzled fans with surprising information. Did you know, for instance, that Merlin had been in

▲
A dragon lords over Gringotts Bank in Diagon Alley at the Wizarding World of Harry Potter in Orlando.

◀
Would-be wizards browse the offerings at Ollivanders' wand shop in the Wizarding World of Harry Potter in Los Angeles (far left). Fans get their thrills at the Orlando theme park (center). Treats galore can be purchased at Honeydukes in L.A. Lead us to the Bertie Bott's Every Flavour Beans (left)!

Slytherin? We didn't.

Rowling also picked up her pen again, writing *The Casual Vacancy* and, under the pseudonym Robert Galbraith, three bestselling detective novels. She was writing for adults, and many of her most faithful readers followed her, even if they still longed for more magic.

They got their wish three years ago. Rowling, it was announced, would provide the story for a stage play that eventually became *Harry Potter and the Cursed Child* and would write the screenplays for a trilogy of spinoff films about Newt Scamander, the fictional author of the Hogwarts textbook *Fantastic Beasts and Where to Find Them*. Just as the original series had evolved over the course of seven books, Rowling is aiming her wand at new territories of the imagination. *Cursed Child* follows Harry, Ron and Hermione into adulthood and chronicles the perils of parenthood and the messes their children get into. *Fantastic Beasts and Where to Find Them*, the first Scamander movie (in theaters November 2016), travels back in time to an era and a continent we've never seen before in the Potter universe: 1920s North America. (New York City, to be more specific.)

But make no mistake: The heart of both new works is pure Rowling. Scamander and Porpentina Goldstein in *Fantastic Beasts*, as well as Albus Severus Potter and Scorpius Malfoy in *Cursed Child*, all learn that friendship and love are more powerful than any of us can imagine. By hopping around her own chronology, Rowling is exploring the nature of time, how we change and what never will—core virtues that have always been a major part of her writing. Her once-in-a-lifetime imagination created not only these fantastical stories but a lens through which to view our own world. *What made 1920s New York different for witches and wizards?* becomes *What excuses do we make for mistreating others?* Behind *What kind of father would Harry Potter be?* lies *What kind of parent will I be?* As exciting as it is—will always be—to discover more about Hogwarts, goblins and spells, these new tales promise even fresh insight into ourselves and the real magic lying within.

▲ Crowds get ready for *Harry Potter and the Cursed Child* outside London's Palace Theatre.

◀ Left to right: Accio!…*Lego Harry Potter* video game. The Sorting Hat beckons in a *Potter* app. Newt Scamander and a Niffler (one of his Fantastic Beasts) in Funko Pop! form. *Inside the Magic: The Making of Fantastic Beasts and Where to Find Them*, one of several new tie-in titles arriving on Muggle bookshelves in November.

**CURTAIN CALL**

# CURSED CHILD

The much-anticipated stage play *Harry Potter and the Cursed Child* opened in London in July 2016. We were there—and were completely, thoroughly enchanted.

The cast of *Harry Potter and the Cursed Child*. Emma Watson meets the play's Hermione, Noma Dumezweni (right).

If ever there were a theater tailor-made for *Harry Potter and the Cursed Child*, it would be the Palace. One of the gems of London's West End, it was built in the late 19th century, and its turreted, red-brick facade looms over the traffic and bustle of Charing Cross Road like an otherworldly apparition. Inside, with its faded beauty, the place recalls Hogwarts: marble and alabaster pillars, sweeping staircases, ornate nooks and crannies of dark wood, a sea of red velvet chairs. Its elegant lobbies and balustrades are swagged with the Hogwarts logo. It looks old. It looks haunted—and it is, according to the program.

The theater is suffused in dim gloom as I take my seat, just a thin pencil of light illuminating an "H" on the dark velvet curtains. A current of anticipation quivers through the crowd. I'm seeing the show in August 2016, just a day after its official opening, and like almost everyone around me, I haven't read the script. I've stayed off social media too, so that not a single aspect of the experience is spoiled for me. Still, as an enormous fan of both the books and the movies, I'm worried that *Cursed Child* will feel like an imposter.

It doesn't. From the very first moment, it's reassuringly familiar. Harry, Ron and Hermione may be adults, but they're still instantly recognizable, and their world is so achingly realized that at times I forget I am at a play. It helps that the special effects are every bit as bewitching as those in the films: Wispy dementors emerge from the ceiling and swoop about the theater, their gauzy ends brushing spectators' heads in the balcony. Wands emit green flashes of fire, blasting various objects across the stage. Characters ingest polyjuice potion and transform, before our eyes, into other people. Halloween lanterns and brooms levitate and fly. A stunning scene unfolds on the roof of the Hogwarts Express as it hurtles through the dark countryside. And in an illusion that truly makes me gasp, characters get sucked dramatically into a phone booth to enter the Ministry of Magic.

It sounds improbable, but in the shadowy glow of the Palace, none of this feels high-tech. What it feels like is, simply, magic. —TINA JORDAN

# J.K.'s Wise Guises

She makes very few public appearances, but fans feel like they know the author thanks to her endlessly amusing Twitter feed. A close look at her 140-or-less missives reveals that they generally fall into five distinct categories. —ISABELLA BIEDENHARN

## EVERYMOM

**@Brocaesar**TV This may get lost in the noise..but what would you say to someone who has failed to find meaning and wants to finally give up?
**@jk_rowling** And I'd say, the world is full of wonderful things you haven't seen yet. Don't ever give up on the chance of seeing them.

**@jk_rowling** I wish I could answer you all but your Tweets come very thick and fast! Be happy & I hereby declare you all cool. X

**@jk_rowling** .@Mattdavelewis I will always support you whatever you want to do, Matthew. Now go put some clothes on.

## COMEDIAN

**@jk_rowling** .@ardit_haliti You think I should write something where nobody dies? Hmm... it wouldn't be easy. I'm all about the death.

**@itssaaaav** what should I do with my life
**@jk_rowling** Ideally, something that makes you happy and doesn't involve serial killing. Can't be more specific without further information.

**@jk_rowling** Pro writing tip: when carrying your open MacBook across a lawn to fetch more tea, do not accidentally activate Photo Booth.

## SOCIAL CRUSADER

**@WBCsigns** So @jk_rowling wants Dumbledore & Gandalf to marry in Ireland; if it happens, WBC will picket! #NotBanned
**@jk_rowling** .@WBCsigns Alas, the sheer awesomeness of such a union in such a place would blow your tiny bigoted minds out of your thick sloping skulls.

**@jk_rowling** I should warn you, I'm a filthy liberal, I used to be very poor and I'm sometimes vulgar enough to mention it

## HARRY POTTER TEAM CAPTAIN

**@jk_rowling** .@m_abs All these people saying they never got their Hogwarts letter: you got the letter. You went to Hogwarts. We were all there together.

**@jk_rowling** There is no equivalence between Hogwarts and Ilvermorny houses, but don't diss Hufflepuff!

**@gillianngracee** It's Draco Malfoy's birthday today, isn't it? (along with my last day of school!) How old would he be turning? xD
**@jk_rowling** Draco turns 35 today. I'm not invited to the party, mainly because I keep telling girls they're misguided to fancy him.

**@jk_rowling** .@HotmHayles Moaning Myrtle's full name was Myrtle Elizabeth Warren.

**@jk_rowling** .@Eowynlily Fred was born first. I always thought that was obvious!

## REGULAR PERSON

**@jk_rowling** Of all devices known to humankind, the desktop printer is the most evil. I am close to breaking point.
**@CanonUKandIE** anything we can do to help?
**@jk_rowling** 'anything we can do to help?' Do you have an exorcist in my area?

**@q_uibbler** you play mine craft? Omg lol
**@jk_rowling** I have an 11 year old son - of course I play Minecraft.
**@anniibl** do you play with the monsters on or off?
**@jk_rowling** On, naturally. I'm hardcore.

**@jk_rowling** When you spend all day creeping past a big dead spider on the floor in case it's only pretending, then realise it's the stalk off a tomato.

**@jk_rowling** And now I'm going to go and cook, which is the perfect antithesis to writing: it's all about the senses, instant gratification and sharing.

J.K. Rowling attends a gala with fans for a performance of *Cursed Child*.


**ENTERTAINMENT WEEKLY**
**Editorial Director** Jess Cagle
**Editor** Henry Goldblatt
**Creative Director** Tim Leong
**Executive Projects Director** Erik Forrest Jackson

**THE ULTIMATE GUIDE TO THE WORLD OF HARRY POTTER AND FANTASTIC BEASTS**
**Editor** Alyssa Smith
**Editor, People + EW Books** Allison Adato
**Designer** Sung Choi
**Photo Editor** Helen Cannavale
**Photo Assistant Editor** Rogelio Esparza
**Writers** Isabella Biedenharn, Christina Cheakalos, Keisha Hatchett, James Hibberd, Jeff Jensen, Tina Jordan, Paul Katz, Stephen King, Chris Nashawaty, Margaret Nelson, Dalton Ross, Sean Smith, Keith Staskiewicz, Kevin Sullivan
**Reporter** Daniel S. Levy
**Copy Desk** Joanann Scali (Chief), James Bradley (Deputy), Ellen Adamson, Gabrielle Danchick, Matt Weingarden (Copy Editors)
**Production Designer** Joni Danaher
**Premedia Executive Director** Richard Prue
**Senior Manager** Romeo Cifelli
**Manager** Rob Roszkowski
**Imaging Production Associate** Jennifer Brown
**Research Director** Céline Wojtala

**TIME INC. BOOKS**
**Publisher** Margot Schupf
**Associate Publisher** Allison Devlin
**Vice President, Finance** Terri Lombardi
**Vice President, Marketing** Jeremy Biloon
**Executive Director, Marketing Services** Carol Pittard
**Director, Brand Marketing** Jean Kennedy
**Finance Director** Kevin Harrington
**Sales Director** Christi Crowley
**Assistant General Counsel** Andrew Goldberg
**Assistant Director, Production** Susan Chodakiewicz
**Senior Manager, Category Marketing** Bryan Christian
**Brand Manager** Katherine Barnet
**Associate Prepress Manager** Alex Voznesenskiy
**Assistant Project Manager for Project Management and Production** Anna Riego

**Editorial Director** Kostya Kennedy
**Creative Director** Gary Stewart
**Director of Photography** Christina Lieberman
**Editorial Operations Director** Jamie Roth Major
**Assistant Art Director** Anne-Michelle Gallero
**Copy Chief** Rina Bander
**Assistant Managing Editor** Gina Scauzillo
**Assistant Editor** Courtney Mifsud

**SPECIAL THANKS & AN ORDER OF MERLIN, FIRST CLASS AWARD**
Brad Beatson, Nicole Fisher, Kristina Jutzi, Seniqua Koger, Nicholas Ritchie, Kate Roncinske, Missy Schwartz





Published by Time Inc. Books
225 Liberty Street
New York, NY 10281





We welcome your comments and suggestions about Entertainment Weekly Books. Please write to us at: Entertainment Weekly Books, Attention: Book Editors, P.O. Box 62310, Tampa, FL 33662-2310
If you would like to order any of our hardcover Collector's Edition books, please call us at 800-327-6388, Monday through Friday, 7 a.m.–9 p.m. Central Time.



**PHOTO CREDITS**
**COVER** Courtesy of Warner Bros. Pictures; **Pg 1:** Courtesy of Warner Bros. Pictures; **Pg 2-3:** Courtesy of Warner Bros. Pictures; **Pg 4-5:** (l-r) John Lamparski/Getty Images; Tim Wimborne/Getty Images; **Pg 6-7:** (clockwise) Daniel Leal-Olivas/Getty Images; AFP/Getty Images, Evan Agostini/Getty Images; **Pg 8-9:** (clockwise) Yeong-Ung Yang/*The New York Times*/Redux; Tobias Schwarz/Reuters/Getty Images; Joe Raedle/Getty Images; **Pg 10-11:** Typographic Illustrations by Edward M. Mann; photo courtesy of Warner Bros. Pictures; **Pg 12-19:** Courtesy of Warner Bros. Pictures; **Pg 24-27:** Courtesy of Warner Bros. Pictures; **Pg 28-29:** Courtesy of Warner Bros. Pictures; **Pg 30-31:** (clockwise) Standard/Rex/Shutterstock; Illustrations by Mary GrandPré © 1998-2007 WBEI. Harry Potter characters, names, and related indicia are trademarks of and © Warner Bros. Entertainment Inc. Harry Potter Publishing Rights © JKR.; Graham Barclay/Getty Images; REX/Shutterstock; AFP/Getty Images; **Pg 32-33:** REX/Shutterstock; Dwayne Senior/eyevine/Redux; Paul Cooper/ REX/Shutterstock; Illustrations by Mary GrandPré © 1998-2007 WBEI. Harry Potter characters, names, and related indicia are trademarks of and © Warner Bros. Entertainment Inc. Harry Potter Publishing Rights © JKR.; Peter Brooker/REX/Shutterstock; Tristan Gregory/Camera Press/Redux; **Pg 33:** *sidebar:* Chris O'Meara/Getty Images; Scholastic(2); **Pg 34-35:** Typographic Illustrations by Edward M. Mann; photo by Mathias Clamer; **Pg 36-37:** Courtesy of Warner Bros. Pictures; **Pg 38-39:** (l-r) Courtesy of Warner Bros. Pictures; *still life*: Dan Winters; **Pg 40-41:** (clockwise) Courtesy of Warner Bros. Pictures; *sidebar*: (l-r) Starstock/Photoshot/Everett Collection; Everett Collection; **Pg 42-43:** Courtesy of Warner Bros. Pictures; **Pg 44-45:** Courtesy of Warner Bros. Pictures; *still life*: Dan Winters; **Pg 46-47:** Courtesy of Warner Bros. Pictures; *sidebar*: prophecy orb; Image provided from The Noble Collection Official Harry Potter licensee for movie props, gifts and collectibles; **Pg 48-49:** Courtesy of Warner Bros. Pictures; **Pg 50-51:** Courtesy of Warner Bros. Pictures; *still life*: Dan Winters; **Pg 52-53:** Courtesy of Warner Bros. Pictures; **Pg 54-55:** Courtesy of Warner Bros. Pictures; **Pg 56-57:** Courtesy of Warner Bros. Pictures; *still life*: Dan Winters; **Pg 58-59:** Courtesy of Warner Bros. Pictures; **Pg 60-61:** Courtesy of Warner Bros. Pictures; **Pg 62-63:** Courtesy of Warner Bros. Pictures; *still life* (3): Dan Winters; **Pg 64-65:** Courtesy of Warner Bros. Pictures; *sidebar*: TM©2003 Fox Broadcasting CR:FOX; TM © 20th Century Fox Film Corp. All rights reserved./Courtesy Everett Collection; TM & © 20th Century Fox Film Corp. All rights reserved./Courtesy Everett Collection; Dana Edelson/NBC; Douglas Gorenstein/NBC/NBCU Photo Bank via Getty Images; Warner Bros./Everett Collection; **Pg 66-67:** Courtesy of Warner Bros. Pictures; **Pg 68-69:** Courtesy of Warner Bros. Pictures; *still life* (2): Dan Winters; **Pg 70-71:** Courtesy of Warner Bros. Pictures; **Pg 72-73:** Courtesy of Warner Bros. Pictures; **Pg 74-75:** Courtesy of Warner Bros. Pictures; **Pg 76-77:** Courtesy of Warner Bros. Pictures; *still life* (2): Dan Winters; Image provided from The Noble Collection Official Harry Potter licensee for movie props, gifts and collectibles (1); **Pg 78-79:** Courtesy of Warner Bros. Pictures; *sidebar*: ©Warner Bros/courtesy Everett Collection / Everett Collection (1); **Pg 82-83:** (clockwise) Dave Hogan/Getty Images; Dave Bennett/Getty Images (2): NBC/Getty Images; Time&Life Pictures/Getty Images: Barry King/Getty Images; **Pg 84-85:** Courtesy of Warner Bros. Pictures (8 portraits); (clockwise) Caitlin Cronenberg/©Entertainment One/Courtesy Everett Collection; Sundance/BBC/Courtesy: Everett Collection; David James/©Lucasfilm 2015/DISNEY; ABC/Richard Cartwright; IndicanPictures; IndicanPictures; Courtesy of Warner Bros. Pictures; Vertical Entertainment/Everett Collection; **Pg 86-87:** Laura Cavanaugh/Getty Images; **Pg 88-89:** Typographic Illustrations by Edward M. Mann; Courtesy of Warner Bros. Pictures; **Pg 90-91:** (clockwise) 2014 Kevin Kolczynski/Universal Orlando; Honeydukes Universal Studios/NBC; Universal Orlando Resort; Emily Berl/The New York Times/Redux; **Pg 92-93:** (clockwise) Nigel Howard/Evening Standard/REDUX; Courtesy of Warner Bros. Entertainment; *sidebar*: Manuel Harlan; Luke Windsor; **Pg 94-95:** Splash Images

PHOTOGRAPH BY HENRIK KNUDSEN

21182250R00055

Printed in Great Britain
by Amazon